The Unburdened Heart

Five Keys to Forgiveness and Freedom

MARIAH BURTON NELSON

HarperSanFrancisco

A Division of HarperCollins*Publishers*

ALSO BY MARIAH BURTON NELSON

*Are We Winning Yet? How Women Are Changing Sports
and Sports Are Changing Women*

*The Stronger Women Get, the More Men Love Football:
Sexism and the American Culture of Sports*

Embracing Victory: Life Lessons in Competition and Compassion

FIRST EDITION

Library of Congress Cataloging-in-Publication Data

Nelson, Mariah Burton.
      The unburdened heart : five keys to forgiveness and freedom \ by Mariah
Burton Nelson.
          p.   cm.
      Includes bibliographical references and index.
      ISBN 0–06–251599–3 (cloth)
      ISBN 0–06–251600–0 (pbk.)
      1. Forgiveness. 2. Nelson, Mariah Burton. 3. Adult child sexual abuse victims.
   I. Title.

BJ1476.N45   2000
179'.9—dc21   99–059763

00   01   02   03   04   ❖/RRD   10 9 8 7 6 5 4 3 2

To Katherine

Contents

PART III: COMPLICATIONS, CLOSURE, AND BEYOND

Preface

Readers who know me as a sportswriter may be wondering: What's forgiveness got to do with sports?

The Unburdened Heart is not a sports story. In that way, it's new territory for me. But I have noticed some similarities between sports and forgiveness. Like the athlete, the forgiver must develop self-awareness and self-discipline. Like the athlete, the forgiver conditions her heart, in a sense, to become stronger and more resilient. And like the athlete, the forgiver achieves her goal slowly, over time, through intention and practice and hard work.

I've written about forgiveness before. Many years ago, I wrote a forgiveness poem called "Conversation Between a Woman and the Man Who Raped Her," which appears for the first time in this book. More recently, in *Embracing Victory: Life Lessons in Competition and Compassion,* I used a basketball metaphor to illustrate this guideline for champions: Forgive yourself immediately for all mistakes.

I've also written previously about Bruce, the coach who molested me—then, twenty years later, apologized, and in that way started me thinking about what it might mean to forgive. I first wrote about him in *The Stronger Women Get, the More Men Love Football,* back when I was furious with him, before I had figured out some things about forgiveness and freedom. Our story is woven throughout this book.

So this book is not a sports book, but it explores themes I've introduced before. And my sports books are not really sports books either. Most of my sports stories are love stories. I believe that through sports, women learn to love themselves, their bodies, and their teammates. I've described competition as a form of love: You love yourself enough to compete for what you want, and you love your opponents because they challenge you to succeed.

More than anything, *The Unburdened Heart* is a love story. It's about the love that becomes available when we lay down the burdens of anger, rage, recrimination, retribution, and superiority.

My sports stories have also been about courage and truth and freedom: the courage to compete, the truth of who female athletes are, the freedom that comes from physical power and teamwork. This book too is about courage, truth, and freedom. Forgiveness is uncharted territory, so it takes courage to go there, risking painful memories, further hurts, and the unpredictable unknown. It requires truth: an honest look at exactly what happened and how it affected everyone involved. And forgiveness leads to freedom, because it results in no longer being defined by or governed by our grievances and grudges. It's about getting past all that, going beyond.

So in a way, this book is a logical progression from my three books about sports and competition. It's another exploration of love, courage, truth, and freedom.

As I've begun to speak about forgiveness in public, people have asked me: "Are you more forgiving than other people?" I don't know. But I do know that I'm more forgiving than I used to be. As I forgave Bruce, and as I read about and wrote about the subject every day, I changed. I started feeling compassion not only for Bruce but for my parents, my siblings, my friends, telemarketers, the drunk driver who rammed into my car, the colleague who doesn't cooperate, the mammography technician who left me standing half-naked in a cold room. I became more accepting of people's idiosyncrasies, their faults, the rude and cruel and criminal things they do. I learned to forgive reflexively, almost automatically, before the other person even has time to apologize. I'm more emotionally generous than before, less judgmental, less arrogant, more ready to assume that all of us are hurting and limited and doing our best, given what we've got. I feel more connected to other people and also more separate: more connected because I remember that we all struggle with emotions, mistakes, failings, and more separate because I'm not taking other people's behavior so personally, even when it involves me. I don't get hurt or insulted as often as before, so there are fewer people on my "to forgive" list. With practice, forgiveness has become a daily habit. And freedom (from guilt, shame, pain, anger, and the pain of constantly criticizing other people) has been the reward.

Most of us have been hurt or exploited or betrayed or bruised or taken advantage of in ways that affect us still—limiting us, impinging on our ability to love ourselves and others. Fortunately, anyone can learn to forgive. It's scary: It takes work, and it generates pain before it eases pain. But it's essential for people who want to stop hurting and hating. It's not just about healing or moving on. It's about growing, emerging freer and happier and more loving than before.

I'm interested in this question: Why forgive?

And this question: How?

This book, to the best of my ability, answers both.

Part I

RISK AND RESISTANCE

Chapter 1

MY YEAR OF FORGIVING DANGEROUSLY

I was fourteen when Bruce started molesting me.[1] He was twenty-five, already a father and coach. The abuse ended three summers later when my family happened to move across the country. The impact of the abuse persisted for more than two decades. Then I wondered, *Might forgiveness be possible?* Then everything changed.

Handsome, witty, and charming, Bruce praised my writing, supported my passion for sports, gave me posters and poetry, and, while I sat frozen in fear and confusion on the car seat next to him, eased his hand inside my sweatpants. I felt deeply flattered, horribly ashamed, guilty, infatuated, scared, and, because he was married, brokenhearted.

Bruce called the behavior "an affair" and complimented me on being "mature enough to handle it." He introduced me to the term "statutory rape," explaining that "other people wouldn't understand—especially your parents," and warning me that if I told anyone, he would go to prison.

About twenty years later, while researching the subject of coach-athlete sexual abuse for a book, I called Bruce out of the blue to interview him. He seemed to welcome the call—our first contact in two decades—saying, "I need to have this conversation too." When I told him how confused and betrayed I had felt, and ashamed of my own "adulterous" behavior, he begged me to forgive him.

"I think I already have forgiven you," I told him. But when I hung up, I felt enraged. I was still furious about the past, I realized, and in a subsequent conversation I rescinded my forgiveness. He called me several more times, "trying to move toward some sort of peace between us." Mistrustful as well as angry, I insisted he stop calling. I concluded our last conversation with a threat: If I found out that he was still molesting girls, I would support those victims in any charges they might bring against him.

My book *The Stronger Women Get, the More Men Love Football* includes a chapter called "My Coach Says He Loves Me." I quoted Bruce but did not name him, still feeling loyal to and ambivalent about a man who had, despite the exploitation, also provided much-needed friendship and mentoring.

Then, in response to requests, I began speaking publicly about coach-athlete abuse—on college campuses, at professional conferences, and on national television. Gradually, I changed my mind about shielding Bruce's identity. *Why should I protect him?* I thought. In some of these appearances, I deliberately used Bruce's name. Though I was not consciously vengeful, anyone might reasonably have interpreted my "outing" him as an expression of revenge.

In December 1996, Bruce called me. My public statements had made their way back to his hometown. His marriage had been shattered. His boss had confronted him and ordered him to be evaluated by a psychiatrist. Now his job was at stake. Again he asked me to forgive him.

"I don't trust you," I said coldly. "You probably just want me to stop identifying you in public."

He told me that he had suffered for many years with guilt and shame. He said he had come close to killing himself—and that he was now considering suicide again. I made a token effort to talk him out of it ("that would be a cruel thing to do to your children") but remained wary and distant, suspecting that he was trying to manipulate me.

Soon afterward, Bruce wrote me a letter explaining that he had confessed all to the psychiatrist and had been cleared to stay at his job. He apologized for having hurt me and invited me to "try to resolve things between us." I didn't respond. Three weeks later, he wrote me a second letter, again apologizing and asking me to consider meeting with him. I read the letters, put them aside, and refocused on my work, my deadlines, my life. I was busy. I was angry. I was wary. *Why should I give him what he wants?* I thought. *Forgiveness is on his agenda, not mine.*

But somewhere deep within, I was touched by his letters. I had to admit, he sounded sincere. He sounded remorseful. Regardless of his motivations, he was reaching out to me, trying to repair a very damaged relationship. It occurred to me: *What if I never forgive him?* At age forty, was I facing another forty years of bitterness over something that had happened in my teens? The wound was not healing on its own. I thought: *Something has to give.* Then I thought: *Maybe that something is me.*

Maybe I could lay down my burden of anger. Maybe, rather than remain forever entrenched in the victim role, I could take responsibility for healing myself. And maybe, in ways I could not yet imagine, Bruce would help me. Twenty-five years after the abuse, the concept of forgiveness began to seem like a remote but appealing possibility.

I called Bruce, saying that "some sort of peace or reconciliation or forgiveness might be possible," adding bitterly, "but I don't see how."

We talked for an hour. The next day I called again and we talked for another hour. Over the next six months, we exchanged many long letters, talked on the phone many times, and met in person twice.

I began to believe that he cared not only about himself but about me. I began to believe that he was telling the truth when he said he had stopped abusing kids more than two decades ago. I began to sense that his request for forgiveness offered me an opportunity: a chance to grow, to learn, and perhaps to heal.

Still, even considering forgiveness felt dangerous. What if he was still molesting girls? What if his sole agenda was to silence me? I was afraid to tell Bruce how I felt, and I was afraid to listen to him. I was afraid to revisit very old, very deep wounds. Expressing anger to him on the phone, I was afraid he would yell at me, threaten me, or even drive to my house and shoot me. When he made little jokes, I was afraid he was trying to seduce me, at least emotionally. Sometimes I felt guilty, the way I had when I was young, as if I were doing something wrong. Sometimes my whole body would shake, as if I were freezing.

I was embarking on a treacherous journey but I was not traveling alone. Bruce, of all people, was accompanying me. Eventually, I thanked him for that: for his active, empathic listening, for the many times he validated my feelings, for his ultimate acceptance of full responsibility.

Though our interactions were tense and difficult, I began to understand his willingness to listen and apologize as a gift—a form of reparations more meaningful to me than any financial settlement we might have agreed to, a form of community service more valuable to me than any jail term he might have endured.

Ultimately, I did forgive him. Then I said good-bye and walked away from a new adult relationship that had become surprisingly tender and fulfilling. The entire process was complex, excruciating, and tremendously sad. It was the most difficult thing I've ever done. It was also extremely liberating.

If that had been all—one person forgiving dangerously—there would have been no book. But along the way, I became a student of forgiveness and learned some things that radically changed my perspective. My journey affected nothing less than the way I see other people, and the way I love. I learned how to confront pain, how to discover compassion for people who hurt me, how to accept people for who they are, even when it's not who I want them to be. I developed humility—and a sense of humor—about my own transgressions. I learned how to forgive myself. And I discovered that forgiveness is a path to freedom.

I sensed I was not alone. There were others who knew what I knew, and more, and I felt compelled to find them. Mark Umbreit, director of the Center for Restorative Justice at the University of Minnesota, spends time in prisons and on death row, serving as a mediator between society's worst criminals and the victims they have left behind. Umbreit says that in his forgiveness work he witnesses "some of the most beautiful aspects of the human experience in the context of some of the most evil." As I researched this topic, I met beautiful, deeply wounded people who shared with me their brave attempts to transcend evil, to reclaim hope and love, and to extend compassion, both to their most hated enemies and to themselves. It was a privilege to witness and only made me more curious about the process of forgiveness: how it happens, and how it affects the forgiver and the forgiven.

By happenstance, my interest in forgiveness paralleled a national and international groundswell of interest in the subject. Almost overnight, forgiveness became a hot topic as political and religious leaders publicly apologized for numerous atrocities. Male athletes from the football player Lawrence Phillips (who assaulted his ex-girlfriend) to the boxer Mike Tyson (who bit his opponent's ear) to the pro basketball player Latrell Sprewell (who choked his coach) made the apology a staple of the sports press conference. The Million Man March and the Promise Keepers' march on Washington emphasized "atonement" for male sins and requests for women's forgiveness. Scientists began studying the relationship between forgiveness and mental health. Archbishop Desmond Tutu established South Africa's Truth and Reconciliation Commission, an unprecedented institutionalization of forgiveness. President Bill Clinton made multiple pleas for forgiveness in regard to his relationship with Monica Lewinsky. Academic conferences explored the subject, the International Forgiveness Institute[2] was founded, the Templeton Foundation offered grants to scholars, numerous movies and books emerged with forgiveness themes, Oprah Winfrey discussed the topic on her show, and columnists in publications as diverse as *Time,* the *Utne Reader,* the *Wall Street Journal, Family Circle,* and *U.S. News & World Report* debated the issue. Teachers, therapists, and families began talking about forgiveness outside of religious settings—which had been the primary context for those discussions for most of human history.

This public fascination with forgiveness is discussed in this book, as are politically motivated apologies. I mention religious doctrine and spiritual tradition. But this book is not about whether grand-scale atrocities such as the Holocaust are forgivable, or whether God forgives us, or whether the United States should apologize to its citizens for such things as slavery. It's a personal book, about human beings who seek to forgive other human beings who have hurt, betrayed, violated, or simply disappointed them. Throughout this book, I weave my personal story: the dramatic and poignant reckoning between molester and molestee. Along the way, I offer many other stories and struggles, along with experts' insights about what happens, or can happen, after abuse, assault, neglect, murder, wrongdoing, affront, or simple misunderstandings.

Unlike other forgiveness books, this book does not advocate a particular religious perspective. Unlike other authors, I do not propose putting limits or conditions on forgiveness ("You should forgive if . . . ," or, "Don't forgive until . . ."). I do not promise or even propose reconciliation; that's a separate consideration. And I do not see forgiveness as an end in itself.

In *The Unburdened Heart*, I offer this observation: Unconditional forgiveness, whether inspired by religious beliefs or not, heals. The one who is healed—the forgiver—becomes free from the pain of the past, and also free to love differently, and love more, in the future. That person may or may not reconcile with the person who hurt them, depending on the needs, interests, and level of trust between those two people. Regardless, forgiveness has widespread personal, interpersonal, and even political ramifications as forgivers begin to treat everyone with more love and compassion.

When I told a friend that I planned to consult a religious leader about forgiveness, she joked, "What are you going to ask: If he's for it or against it?"

We laughed. Of course he would be "for" it. And he was.

But it's one thing to be "for" forgiveness—who isn't?—and quite another to integrate it into your life.

"Everyone says forgiveness is a lovely idea until they have something to forgive," noted C. S. Lewis.[3]

Usually forgiveness does not happen immediately. It requires time and thought. Usually forgiveness is not easy. Otherwise, more people would do it. Forgiveness can involve confusion and anger and a deep grieving that you didn't feel originally, when the hurt first occurred. Often you must forgive repeatedly, for the same offense. It's not simple.

But it's essential. "Without forgiveness," the philosopher Hannah Arendt noted, "we would never be released from the consequences of what we have done or what has been done to us, and our capacity to act would, as it were, be confined to one single deed from which we could never recover."[4]

"Without forgiveness," said Archbishop Desmond Tutu, "there would be no future."[5]

Almost all religions advocate some aspects of forgiveness. The New Testament tells Christians to forgive. The Koran tells Muslims to forgive. Judaism institutionalizes atonement. Buddhism recommends compassion for all living things. The Hindu Bhagavad Gita says, "If you want to see the brave, look at those who can forgive. If you want to see the heroic, look at those who can love in return for hatred."

Forgiveness is integral to most Native American religions. The Seneca Indian writer José Hobday says he learned about forgiveness from his mother, who would say to him when he was sought revenge: "Do not be so ignorant and stupid and inhuman as they are. Go to an elder and ask for the medicine that will turn your heart from bitterness to sweetness. You must learn the wisdom of how to let go of the poison."[6]

Despite agreement that we should be "for" forgiveness, how and when and what to forgive are widely debated and disputed issues. Jews and Christians disagree. Feminists and psychologists disagree. And most experts disagree with the dictionary. So when President Clinton asked for forgiveness, it wasn't clear whether he was asking people to pardon his behavior, as the dictionary indicates, or to "decrease resentment toward and increase compassion toward" him, as the president of the International Forgiveness Institute, Robert Enright, defines the term, or simply to reward him with political absolution so he could remain in office, as many cynical constituents suspected.

There are those who say that regardless of apologies and contrition and other offerings, we must not forgive Clinton, or many other people, because to forgive is to condone reprehensible behavior. According to this view, forgiveness sends the wrong message: The offender's behavior wasn't wrong after all.

Other people believe that forgiveness should be granted only if certain conditions are met, including any or all of these: admission, apology, atonement, reparations, and contrition. Hence, President Clinton's speech admitting an "improper relationship" with Lewinsky was criticized as insufficiently contrite. News accounts noted that he did not utter the words *sorry* or *apology*. In his subsequent requests for forgiveness, he used those words repeatedly.

But forgiveness should not be used as a bargaining chip to control someone who misbehaved ("If you jump through these hoops, I'll forgive you"). We shouldn't relinquish control to them like that, leaving our forgiveness in their hands.

Nor should forgiveness be seen as synonymous with pardoning, except in the sense of forgiving a financial debt. Forgiveness and justice are separate issues, and not incompatible. You can forgive someone and still press charges against them. If you want to prevent that person from hurting others, lock the door to the jailhouse, or lock the door to your own house. But keep the doors to your heart open.

Forgiveness does not mean condoning, though many people think it does. To condone is to excuse, tolerate, overlook, or disregard an offense. It implies that the offense is trivial or harmless. But someone who is considering forgiveness is doing so precisely because they do not excuse or minimize the offense and do not perceive it to be trivial. They have suffered. Otherwise, forgiveness would not be necessary.

Forgiveness does not mean martyrdom. Forgiveness does not mean forgetting. Forgiveness does not guarantee trust or reconciliation. After forgiveness, we shouldn't continue being abused or betrayed or used or mocked or insulted. We can forgive and also say no. We can forgive and file for divorce.

The word *forgive* comes from Middle English words meaning "before" and "gift." So maybe it's a gift in response to what came before. Or a gift before any such gift is expected. Many people have said forgiveness is a gift you give yourself, because you'll feel better, and that's true. It's primarily for you. But it's also a gift to the person who hurt you, because you can relieve them of some of their guilt or shame. And it's a gift to your friends and family and acquaintances because when the doors of your heart open, they open in all directions, freeing you to become a much more loving, compassionate person.

Forgiveness is a choice. We can't necessarily forgive just because we want to, but even asking the question *Might I forgive?* can subtly open possibilities. We can also choose not to forgive. Framing it as a choice helps bring it to a conscious level.

Forgiveness is empowering. Many of us believe that our own happiness cannot be achieved until someone else comes crawling to us on hands and knees, or learns their lesson, or promises to be different. But our happiness is not really dependent on the behavior of other people. The forgiver changes her focus from *If only they would . . . ,* to *I wonder if I could. . . .*

Forgiveness is a skill. Like shooting basketballs through a hoop, it gets easier with practice. Some people recommend practicing first on the easy stuff: forgiving a grumpy child, an incompetent receptionist, a nosy neighbor. But sometimes the "hard stuff" becomes the training ground because it demands attention, as Bruce demanded mine. Either way, for-givers improve with repeated efforts, with a commitment to learning every detail of how the process works, and with the application of for-giveness skills to new situations.

Forgiveness is a journey. It requires endurance and a willingness to face the unknown. The key is "to begin and to continue," says the author Clarisa Pinkola Estés.[7]

Forgiveness is also, it seems to me, a sixth stage of grief. Elisabeth Kubler-Ross identified denial, anger, bargaining, depression, and accep-tance as the five stages of grieving (or dying, or loss). Forgiveness is what you do after acceptance, when acceptance is not enough, when you've lost something important—a relationship, a dream, a self-image, a physical ability—and you still feel empty or bitter inside. You start forgiving the other person for dying, or for leaving you, or for injuring your elbow, or for saying those mean things many years ago. You start forgiving yourself for not having been a better friend or spouse or daughter or employee. Forgiveness completes the grieving process, allowing you not only to "move on" but to become stronger, more generous, and more loving.

I take this radical stance: Forgiveness is advisable even if offenders never admit culpability and never offer reparations of any kind. Even if they don't admit that they hurt you, or don't care that you're hurt, or pre-tend the incident never happened. Even if they blame you, or won't talk to you, or have long since died. Forgive anyway, regardless of what the other person says or does. Forgive when you're unsure, or afraid, or resentful, or wanting to exact revenge. Forgive when the other person doesn't apologize, or doesn't apologize correctly. Forgive them for that: for their inability, unwillingness, stubbornness, fear.

I'm proposing a departure from the usual ways of dealing with pain: unending blame, anger, bitterness, and quid pro quo ("I'll forgive you only if . . ."). I'm advocating what Jesus, the most radical of forgivers, was advocating when soldiers were hammering huge pointed spikes through his hands, then hoisting his cross. "Forgive them, Father, they know not what they've done," he said. His murderers had not apologized. They didn't use the word *sorry.* Yet even then, in the midst of his own execu-tion, Jesus had forgiveness on his mind.

Here's how unconditional forgiveness works: When the forgiver hears no apology, she recognizes the other person's limitations, remembering how difficult it can be for many of us to take responsibility, even for small transgressions. When she hears an apology but it doesn't sound sufficient, she imagines how hard it must be for someone else to apologize in just the way she wants. She forgives them for what they did and also for what they cannot or will not do. She stops waiting for her offender to do anything at all. She stops blaming someone else for her unhappiness. She stops focusing on the past and starts taking responsibility for the future. She stops singing the "you done me wrong" blues and starts vocalizing her own plans. And she stops feeling superior to others and remembers her own frailty and failings.

It is possible to heal without forgiveness. "Letting go" is the process of allowing your negative feelings and attachments to abate. The offender need not be involved, in actuality or in your mind. You can use prayer, or meditation, or determination, or sometimes simply the healing power of time to get past anger, bitterness, and vindictiveness. For some people this works, and for some people this is enough.

Forgiveness, by contrast, involves thinking about the other person and wondering why they did what they did. You won't necessarily comprehend how it happened. You won't necessarily ask them or tell them about your process. That person might not be available to discuss it with you. But the offender is taken into consideration. In that way, forgiveness always involves more than one person. It's a relationship. It's the generous act of welcoming an offender back into your heart.

How can I propose unconditional forgiveness when, in my own experience, I placed certain conditions on Bruce? *You must apologize, you must take full responsibility, and you must convince me you're not currently molesting girls.* Am I suggesting to readers that they should forgive unconditionally though I did not?

No. I'm suggesting that we all could forgive unconditionally—and that it's often our only choice. Of course, apologies and other indications of remorse and support are preferable to denial, blame, or silence. But I'm less concerned with what's preferable and more concerned with what's real: imperfect human beings stumbling along, hurting each other, and seeking ways to mend. In reality, many people never receive the kind of apology they seek.

In my case, Bruce gave me many things, but he didn't give me everything I wanted. For instance, he refused to "come out" in public as a child molester, as I had requested, claiming that the members of his community would never accept him if they knew. He refused to read the chapter I had written on coach-athlete abuse, claiming that he wasn't strong enough to withstand seeing my anger at him in print. He complicated matters by threatening to commit suicide, by telling me about his unrelated family problems, and by implicitly asking me to fulfill some of his emotional needs—all of which had the effect of eliciting both my sympathy and my anger. I ended up forgiving him for all of that too.

Early in my research, the father of a murdered child asked me, "Do you think the forgiveness process is the same for small things and big things?"

The answer seemed obvious at first: Only a fool would equate a paper cut with a knife wound, a fender bender with a fatal accident. Surely the forgiveness process must be slower, more difficult, and more complicated when the scale of pain and loss and injury is great.

But now I've met people who harbored hatred for decades over simple slights, and I've met people who instantly forgave criminals for felony offenses. I've noticed that some people are more easily and more deeply hurt than others, regardless of how small or large the transgression. Some feel more incensed by an arrogant sales clerk than others might feel after being mugged.

One difference is that huge offenses sometimes raise the question of forgiveness in a way the tiny offenses do not. If your neighbor argues with you about where you park your car, you can hold a grudge against that person all your life, recounting the story of the dispute to anyone who will listen, but unless you're an unusually sensitive person, the level of anger you're feeling won't affect your ability to love others, or celebrate life, or sleep well at night, at least not in ways you'll notice. However, if that neighbor sets fire to your house, your level of rage and your sense of violation may be so tremendous that your pain may consume you, destroying all hope and joy, until you ask yourself: *Might I be able to forgive?*

In this book, I include stories about everyday annoyances and stories about almost unimaginable crimes. These offenses are not the same, of course. Nor do I mean to equate anyone's forgiveness process with any-one else's. Those of us who forgive do so in our own unique way. Yet I hope to provide guidance for anyone who wants to forgive, regardless of the magnitude of the offenses committed and regardless of the magni-tude of their pain.

In the five central chapters of this book, I offer five keys to forgiveness and freedom. Originally, I thought of them as simply keys to forgiveness, but now my goal has changed, along with my sense of what's possible. I had thought that forgiveness was the destination, but now I see that it's only a vehicle that carries us to the destination, which is freedom.

Like Kubler-Ross's five stages of grief, my five keys to forgiveness and freedom are neither linear nor necessarily within conscious control. Some have emotional components that cannot be rushed or forced. How or if they happen may vary according to your motivation to stop hurting, whatever assistance you receive from the perpetrator, and other individ-ual factors. In some situations, only a few of the keys are necessary; other situations require all five. But these seem to be the essential keys.

Awareness The first defense against pain is denial: *It didn't happen. . . . It wasn't important. . . . It didn't affect me much. . . . They didn't mean it, and therefore I shouldn't be angry.* It's often much more comfortable to stay in denial than to face what actually occurred. Yet forgiveness cannot take place unless you decide *who* you are forgiving, and *what* you are forgiv-ing that person *for.* What happened? Who was responsible? What were the consequences? How did you feel about it then, and how do you feel about it now? What impact did it have on how you see yourself and the world? This process of remembering and acknowledging exactly what happened can take courage, since it can rip apart old wounds. Answers to these questions can be surprising and unwelcome. Maybe, when you really think about it, what you remember wasn't quite the same as what happened. Maybe the person who seemed to be at fault really wasn't, or not entirely. Yet without directly addressing the problem, its conse-quences, and the emotional repercussions, forgiveness has no meaning.

Validation We are a species of storytellers. It's through talking and lis-tening to each other that we grow, heal, and understand ourselves and each other. After becoming aware of what happened—or as part of that process—the potential forgiver generally shares her story with someone else. The simple act of talking, and feeling heard, can help ease the burden of anger. If the offender will listen sympathetically, that's ideal. If not, friends, therapists, support groups, e-mail discussion groups, or other sympathetic people can validate that something hurtful happened; that it was not your imagination; that you are not wrong to be grieving, or enraged, or afraid, or simply hurt.

Compassion Though initially inconceivable, compassion for the offender is an essential step toward forgiveness. Compassion for yourself comes first: taking care of your wounds and seeking help from those who can validate, listen, and nurture. Then, when you can begin to inch beyond your own pain, seeking compassion for the offender becomes key. People hurt others because they themselves are hurting—or confused or ignorant. Thus, offenders are candidates for compassion—for their own pain, confusion, and ignorance, present and past. Even murderers, rapists, and terrorists—perpetrators of crimes so heinous they stun the rest of us— these people too could be said to "deserve" compassion, for the simple and obvious fact that they have suffered. Otherwise, they would not have done what they did. South Africans call this process "seeking the humanity in others" *(ubuntu)*. As you seek someone else's humanity, you rediscover your own.

Humility Somewhere along the way, as the rage subsides, we remember that we're not only victims. We have hurt other people ourselves, whether through insensitivity, misguided intentions, or malicious acts. Humility helps place our own injuries into context, locating them somewhere in the broad range of human experience. As we take stock of our own frailties, faults, and failings, we begin to feel less victimized, and less different from the offender. Once we are in touch with our own shortcomings, the question arises: Can we forgive ourselves?

Self-Forgiveness This is the process of giving ourselves permission to be who we are. Like forgiving others, self-forgiveness is a gift, a demonstration of compassion for the person who often needs it most. It's essential for people who believe they somehow participated in getting injured, it's good practice for learning to forgive others, and it's perhaps the most important aspect of forgiveness, since many of us are more critical of ourselves than we are of anyone else.

Awareness, validation, compassion, humility, and self-forgiveness are keys that open the doors to the heart. Once your heart is open, you're free from carting around old gripes and grudges. You're free from the past. You're free from the person who wounded you in the past, and free to let go of the identity of victim or martyr. You're free from the long wait to hear "I'm sorry." You're free to rebuild a relationship with the person who hurt you, or not. You're free to love more, and to receive more love.

This is what freedom looks like: a place beyond ego, where you realize that what other people are doing is not really about you at all. Things that had seemed unforgivable affronts to your dignity and self-respect become pitiable, but no longer personal. You feel injured, insulted, offended, and betrayed less often, so the whole struggle with hurt, anger, vindictiveness, and forgiveness becomes moot.

Well, not entirely. Even people with airy, wide-open hearts still get their feelings hurt, and blame people, and grow resentful, and need to forgive repeatedly. Forgiveness is not the idealized, divine virtue that is preached from the pulpit, but a messy, painful, awkward, difficult dance between fallible and wounded human beings.

The primary message of the book is this: Forgiveness is a viable option for people who want to stop hurting and hating. It takes work; it generates pain before it eases pain; it's scary; it involves acknowledging your own flaws and failings; it's not always politically popular.

But it's freeing.

Chapter 2

WHY PEOPLE DON'T FORGIVE

I didn't forgive Bruce for more than two decades because it never occurred to me as an option. Then, once I started exploring the possibility, I didn't know how, or what it might mean. Were there certain steps that I should take, or that he should? Where would we begin? I had numerous doubts and fears. Might I be "letting him off the hook"? Would he manipulate my emotions—again? Was it worth the risk? How would I feel during the process? How would I feel afterward? How might it influence my life, or his?

Though *forgive* is a common word, it's not what we generally think of first when we're insulted or hurt. If the question *Should I forgive?* comes up at all, it's usually an afterthought, one that arises long after our anger has solidified and begun to take a toll on our emotions, or blood pressure, or worldview. During a fight with a lover, many of us hurl all our past grievances at that person because we haven't done what I think of as forgiveness homework. We haven't consciously forgiven our partner for past injuries. The old wounds remain unhealed.

We don't often discuss the complexities, challenges, and ramifications of forgiveness. Outside of religious contexts, we don't discuss it much at all, beyond simple statements like, "I couldn't possibly forgive her for that," or, "I hope he forgives me." Some of the people I interviewed qualified their answers with: "It depends on what you mean by forgive." When asked to define it themselves, they struggled.

In a class I taught at the Washington Ethical Society, I asked the students, all adults, to define forgiveness in their own words. Categorizing their responses, I found that half defined it in terms of their own feelings ("letting go of anger," "letting go of negative feelings," "peace of mind"), and the other half defined it in terms of a relationship with another person ("not holding something against someone," "not making the other person 'wrong' anymore," "achieving a comfortable new relationship"). So we don't seem to share a common understanding of what it means to forgive.

Another time, after I gave a speech to a group of teenagers in New Mexico, a teacher in the back of the room stood up during the question-and-answer period and said angrily, "My father molested me. I'm never going to forgive him, and I resent your telling me I should."

I nodded, not knowing what else to do. Then one of the teenagers in the front row raised her hand, stood, and turned to face the teacher. "She's not telling you that you should forgive," she explained. "She's just saying that if you do, your heart will open."

The teenager was right. I'm not telling anyone they should forgive. In fact, there are a lot of good reasons why people don't forgive. Not forgiving is the "logical, appropriate, instinctive, normal, natural, and proper response to offenses and hurts," Doris Donnelly wrote in *Learning to Forgive*. It "honors emotions, it affirms rather than denies pain and its after-effects, and it looks after the person who was so damaged in the scuffle."[1]

But after a while, the person damaged in the scuffle isn't really looked after so much as burdened. It's painful to nurse a grudge, to grow angry every time someone's name is mentioned, to reexperience an injury over and over and over again. Anger can be energizing, but when anger ferments into bitterness, it can be debilitating.

When I interviewed people who had not forgiven, they frequently interviewed me in return, searching for a way to see things differently, a way to forgive despite their belief that they couldn't or shouldn't. "How can I forgive when the other person hasn't even apologized?" they often asked. It was an explanation of their nonforgiveness, but also a sincere question, a plea for help.

Forgiving is a journey into the unknown, and anyone who has traveled even partway down that path knows that it may include shame, guilt, painful memories, or a risky confrontation with the one who inflicted the original wound. That's why people say, "Oh, I've let it go," when they really haven't. It's easier, apparently, to convince ourselves that we have forgiven than to remember everything, diving into the muck of memories, emotions, and complex relationships.

So the person who has been hurt chooses between two unappealing options. On the one hand, she can make the costly choice to stay chronically angry. On the other hand, she can embark on an uncharted journey toward forgiveness, a process that can be long, arduous, and even nauseating, exacting its own price. Many times, we choose to stay where we are, preferring the known to the unknown.

I've identified several common reasons why people don't forgive. These are good, rational reasons, and I'm sure there are more; the exact number is unimportant. I discuss these reasons because I think it's important to show how defended we are when it comes to forgiveness. I also want to show how natural it is not to forgive. There's nothing wrong with us for not forgiving.

WE LACK EXPERIENCE AND EXPERTISE

Who teaches us how to forgive? How many of us study it in school? How many parents sit with their children at bedtime and review the day's events, apologizing for their own mistakes and helping children do the same? We teach kids to say, "I forgive you," after someone says, "I'm sorry," but usually it's rote, like "please" and "thank you." Without having practiced forgiveness, we don't know how to go about it. We hesitate because we believe we can't do it, or we don't know how it may affect our lives.

WE'RE ANGRY

"I'm still too angry to forgive," people tell me, or, "I can't forgive him. He's an idiot." Anger is important—for a while. When the pain is new, the prospect of forgiveness can be premature. Anger demonstrates that we were hurt and gives us something to do besides feel the despair, hopelessness, or wrenching pain that can accompany a betrayal or loss.

Anger also motivates political action, which can generate a sense of purpose, perhaps toward preventing future abuses or betrayals. Anger can be pleasurable, as demonstrated by the movie industry's success in exploiting the popular themes of revenge and retaliation.

Often, however, anger masks hurt. As long as we act angry, we keep other people at bay, thus protecting ourselves from the risks of intimacy with those who might hurt us again. And as long as we're raging against someone else, identifying them as the source of our pain, we're not dwelling on our own vulnerability.

Anger also deflects attention away from our shame, maintaining an illusion of goodness and moral superiority, distracting us from thinking about our own flaws. Even our bad moods, poor judgments, addictions, obsessions, and unkind words or deeds can be blamed on an original injurer. It's easy to accuse someone else of causing our bad behavior and unhappiness. How much harder to take responsibility for our own actions and outlook.

WE'RE AFRAID OF BEING HURT AGAIN

When you risk forgiveness, you risk feeling more: more love, but also more sadness, empathy, longing, grief, tenderness. You risk changing your worldview as you develop more compassion for other people, and for yourself. You risk becoming a different sort of person. The big risk is that you will change, and change itself is usually scary, because it means venturing into the unknown.

In my adult contact with Bruce, I was aware of two risks: physical and emotional. I did not fear him sexually. I knew I would not allow myself to be seduced again, and there was never any reason to think he would sexually attack me. But he told me that he was suicidal and admitted that he kept a gun by his bedside. When we began to discuss the possibility of a face-to-face meeting, I insisted he get rid of the gun.

He groaned. "You don't think I'd harm you more than I already have, do you?"

"I don't know you, Bruce," I replied bluntly. "I read all the time about angry men shooting women." He did not seem violent, but I didn't want to have to worry about either of two scenarios: that he would kill me or that he would kill himself. I told him I'm afraid of guns—as indeed I am—and that I did not want him to die.

The next time we talked, he said he had donated the gun to a local police department. Though I couldn't verify that he was telling the truth, he seemed to be. "I know you were concerned about your own safety, but it meant a lot to me that you also wanted me to live, after how much I hurt you," he said.

My other fear was for my emotional safety. In a letter to Bruce, I wrote:

> This feels like a huge risk: reestablishing contact with you. Why? Because I'm starting to trust that you do care, not only about yourself but about me, and I'm starting to trust that you are telling me the truth. To trust is to be vulnerable; to be vulnerable is to create a situation in which I could be hurt again; to be re-hurt and re-betrayed by you would be devastating as well as foolish. I'm trying to be cautious, but it's not really my nature.
>
> One friend, when I told her what I'm doing and that it feels risky, said, "Yes, it's risky, but it's also risky not to change, to let the pain and anger continue to affect your life negatively."

Bruce responded, in part:

> Your friend sounds wise in her understanding of risk. I recognize this and applaud your willingness to attempt the process. I also believe that to find forgiveness and peace is the only way to live the remainder of our lives with an appreciation for all that it can offer.

WE'VE GROWN COMFORTABLE IN THE VICTIM ROLE

We all know at least one professional victim. She takes everything personally, remembers every slight, and eagerly tells everyone all about it. At any opportunity, she recounts in detail the story of the cab driver who gave her the wrong change, the friend who told an off-color joke in front of her kids, the boss who never thanked her after all she did for him and then had the audacity to begrudge her a day off when her father needed a ride to his chemotherapy treatments. No matter that these events may have happened eons ago. They generate new resentment with every telling.

All of us do this to some extent. We've all got our pet grudges, the people we have never forgiven for one thing or another. We get energized by talking about the grievances; we welcome new audiences; we are revitalized by our sense of indignation: *How could that person do that to me?* It can become rewarding, this victim stance. It gives us an identity—one who was wounded—and this identity can grow comfortable, familiar. It can become part of who we are, how we see the world, how we think about and talk about other people. John Landi, a therapist in private practice in Centerville, Virginia, asks, "Is the trauma giving you an identity? If so, you're not going to give it up easily."

OUR CULTURE DOESN'T EMPHASIZE FORGIVENESS

Our culture offers a lot of support for victimhood, martyrdom, and vengeance—often more than it does for charity and compassion. "I wish I could strangle him" is more likely to elicit a sympathetic response than "I'm willing to welcome him back into my heart."

Eleanor, the widow of a famous jazz musician, grew up in a small town in Europe, "where the average person does not have an unforgiving value system," she recalls. "I was astonished when I first came here and people were talking about the death penalty, or applauding life imprisonment. The whole idea of getting revenge seems a very American part of life, the settling of things by guns and might. Even in cartoons, there's all that violence and revenge, so much satisfaction in getting back at people."

WE DON'T WANT TO ADMIT THAT WE WERE HURT

Walking my dog in the neighborhood, I strike up a conversation with a man rebuilding a fence. He and his neighbor had a dispute about the height of this fence, he explains. Angry words were exchanged. Now he must lower it to meet the local code. He's still enraged at the neighbor for insisting he meet this code.

"Fences like this are hard to fix," he tells me.

I nod. "Relationships are even harder to fix," I offer. *This is none of my business,* I realize as soon as I've said it, but I've got forgiveness on my mind.

He glances at the house next door. "Oh, I don't care about that old geezer," he replies. "The damage has been done."

Apparently the fence fight is unforgivable. Irreparable damage has been done. But I don't believe that he doesn't care. His angry tone tells me that he does. I bet the "old geezer" said something hurtful to this younger man, who won't admit that because it would make him feel too vulnerable. Instead, he'll probably seethe on a daily basis, year after year, while he and the old man shovel their parts of their shared sidewalk and drag their trash cans to the ends of their parallel driveways. Will this man ever identify his bitterness as his own problem, I wonder, or will he always blame his neighbor?

To forgive, we have to admit that we do care—that we got our feelings hurt, and that our feelings matter. We have to take responsibility for repairing relationships, when possible, or at least repairing our own hearts, rather than simply rejecting or disliking the person who offended us. All of which is far more difficult than building fences.

We Fool Ourselves into Thinking We Have Already Forgiven

The first time Bruce asked me to forgive him and I responded, "I think I already have forgiven you," I was wrong. I hadn't yet done the work. I wasn't aware of my own feelings, or the consequences of the abuse, or even exactly what had happened. No one had listened to my experiences or validated my pain. I hadn't developed any insight into or compassion for Bruce's life experience. I had zero humility about my own numerous misdeeds. Nor had I forgiven myself for having been young and naive.

In my interviews, I met other people who were doing this: pretending to have forgiven because they felt like they should have done so, or wanted to, but in fact they hadn't. Denial is a psychological defense mechanism that blocks pain by avoiding the truth. One way to avoid the truth is to assert quickly that forgiveness has already been granted—before the difficult, messy work has actually begun. Another way is to pretend the incident didn't happen.

Still in denial about the damage Bruce had inflicted, I somehow figured I must have automatically forgiven him somewhere along the way. The concept of "automatic" forgiveness for felonious criminal behavior did not strike me as absurd. I didn't know that you can't forgive if you haven't yet comprehended the injury. You can't go directly from "nothing bad happened" to "I forgive you"—because in that case there would be nothing to forgive.

Religious leaders have warned against false forgiveness. One of Saint Benedict's injunctions was "never to give a false peace."[2] But apparently a false peace is common. Peter Rutter noted in *Sex in the Forbidden Zone* that "many women are so anxious to put a sexual-boundary violation behind them that at the slightest show of contrition they prematurely forgive or reconcile with the man who has injured them."[3]

Perpetrators can play into this, demanding instant forgiveness. Becky Palmer, a therapist and director of programs and administration at the Center for Contextual Change in Skokie, Illinois, says that sex offenders "always want forgiveness, and they always want it right away," long before they have admitted exactly what they did wrong, and long before they have engaged in a healing relationship with their victim.

When I said to Bruce, "I think I already have forgiven you," I didn't even understand what the concept meant. But I wanted to leapfrog over the process, avoid any conflict, and arrive at that comfortable place of resolution: It's all over now.

WE DON'T WANT TO LOOK IN THE MIRROR

Thoughtless people remind us of our own thoughtlessness—which we'd rather not think about! So we focus on how inconsiderate they are, and how unfair they are to us.

At least, I do this. I hate people whose behavior reminds me of the things I hate about myself. When I can't forgive, often it's because someone is acting too much like I act when I'm on my worst behavior, or too much like I used to act when I was younger, or too much like I would act if I weren't so vigilant. I find another person's behavior unforgivable because I can't forgive it in myself. The dull dinner guest who talks in a nonstop monotone, for instance, may become a target of my wrath (especially if they're talking to me) because I'm afraid of boring people and hence monitor my speech accordingly. Watching someone else engage in the very behavior I would hate in myself makes me hate them—at least until I remember what's going on.

Our Egos Get in the Way

"I have often said, 'I forgive you,' but even as I said these words my heart remained angry or resentful," admitted the priest and author Henri Nouwen. "I still wanted to hear the story that tells me that I was right after all; I still wanted to hear apologies and excuses; I still wanted the satisfaction of receiving some praise in return—if only the praise for being so forgiving!"[4]

To forgive is to let go of all that, and more. Naturally, we want to be right, to be appreciated, to receive something in return for our generous gift. But forgiveness means letting go of ego: the blame, the grudges, the notion that we are superior, even the account books that keep score of who is cruel (bad) and who is forgiving (good).

We Want to Stay Connected to the One Who Hurt Us

Not forgiving keeps us in a relationship with the person who disappointed us, betrayed us, didn't love or honor us the way we wanted them to. Through our rage or hatred, we get to keep thinking about that parent or spouse or former friend and maintain a relationship with them, even if we no longer have actual contact.

Sometimes, through this connection, we hope to teach the other person a lesson. We may persist in suffering to prove that we were wronged, or that we didn't deserve to be treated that way. We may try to motivate the one who hurt us to "earn" our forgiveness—hoping we can induce them not only to apologize but also to behave better in the future. We may wield nonforgiveness as a weapon, wanting the other person to suffer. Becky Palmer notes that in the case of sexual abuse "not forgiving is often the only punishment meted out to offenders." Naturally, then, people use nonforgiveness as a way to "withhold something from this person who has taken so much from them."

Here's the trade-off: Nonforgiveness allows us to stay emotionally involved with someone from the past but prevents us from connecting with people in the present. "I've seen so many people—friends and patients—who 'embrace' a loathed and never-forgiven person so ardently that they squeeze out any room in their own heart to love other people," says Ann Rasmussen, a clinical psychologist from Arlington, Virginia. "So much of their vital energy is spent harboring, feeding, and talking about their resentment. Often people hate their parents for their transgressions three or more decades ago. The tragedy is that they wall their hearts off from new love that could heal them."

WE THINK THE PERSON DOESN'T DESERVE FORGIVENESS

A seventy-four-year-old environmental activist tells me that she won't forgive her first husband because "he betrayed and lied to everybody. We had four children, in four years, a nice life. I'd take off my apron by the time he got home so things would be nice. I'd entertain his friends on weekends, take them to football games. I'd say, 'Be quiet children, Daddy needs his martini.' I gave up a college education. You would think that would be enough. But he had a lover. She was an airline hostess, fifteen years younger. I didn't know about it for thirty years. I was feeling sorry for him that he was working so late."

He lied about his salary too, she says. "He'd say, 'I have no money,' and I believed that until finally his salary was published in the newspaper. His own son says he's a sociopath. He tried to ruin our lives. After the divorce, he wouldn't send money. I was trying to raise the children, get them educated, get them to the dentist. We couldn't even afford movies, and he was making $125,000 per year."

She's not interested in forgiveness, she says, because he doesn't deserve it. She doesn't believe in forgiving people who don't change and don't apologize. "Do you go around forgiving everyone who lashes out at you? That's ridiculous," she says.

THE OFFENDER DOESN'T APOLOGIZE

Apologies can be so healing—when they happen. When they don't happen, many of us get stuck in lifelong bitterness. Donna, a victims' advocate in Abbot, Maine, has never forgiven her mother for not sending her to college. She says it's "impossible because she will not admit she did anything wrong." Though Donna was an honor-roll student in high school, her mother opposed college because she believed her daughter would "just run off and get married," recalls Donna.

"I could understand if they couldn't afford college, but my father was a truck driver with the Teamsters. Mom worked in an office. They could afford it," contends Donna, now in her late forties. She "saw college as a chance to get an education, meet people, get away from the nest at home." Instead, she worked as a stenographer and took college courses on her own but married young, had children early, and never graduated. "My mother cheated me," she says.

Nor has Donna forgiven her mother for not supporting her interest in sports. "In my high school, there were no sports programs for girls. A couple of years later, some parents went to the administration and asked about it. Then there were programs, just like that. Why didn't my parents do that? Sports would have given me a group to belong to. I'm fairly athletic. One time I got on a softball team, but Mother wouldn't drive the ten miles to practice."

Forgiving her mother regarding either college or sports is not possible, Donna says, "because she won't apologize. She won't even admit she was wrong. I know if I confronted her, she would come up with excuses." When Donna raised the subject of the softball team a few years ago, her mother "denied that it ever happened."

"I'll probably go to my grave without forgiving her," Donna predicts.

WE BELIEVE THE APOLOGY ISN'T SINCERE

Sometimes people choose not to forgive in protest of facile apologies. The former Dallas priest Rudolph Kos allegedly sexually assaulted eleven boys hundreds of times over an eleven-year period, until he was suspended in 1992. The diocese was ordered by a jury to pay almost

$120 million in damages to the former altar boys and the parents of one victim, Jay Lemberger, who had committed suicide.

In 1997 a Dallas bishop publicly apologized to the ten surviving victims and the parents of the one who died, on behalf of Rudolph Kos. "I feel the pain that has been part of their lives over these years," said Bishop Charles Grahmann. "I want them to be healed and all of us to be reconciled with each other."

"I'm afraid he's using this as a tool to win back the public," said Wade Schlosstein, one of the victims. One of the men's attorneys called the bishop's action a callous public relations exercise.[5]

Mitchell Johnson's apology was also rejected. He and Andrew Golden killed four classmates and a popular teacher outside their school in Jonesboro, Arkansas, on March 24, 1998. Found guilty of capital murder, they were sentenced to a state detention center until their twenty-first birthdays.

Moments before being sentenced, Johnson, on his fourteenth birthday, read this statement in court: "I understand that it may be impossible for some of you to forgive me. If I could go back and change what happened . . . I would in a minute. I really thought that no one would be hurt. I felt that we would shoot over everyone's heads."

Mitchell Wright, whose wife, Shannon, was killed while saving the life of one of her students, responded, "There is no satisfaction. When I looked that boy [Johnson] in the eye, he didn't look like he was very sorry to me."[6]

WE WAIT FOR THE WRONGDOER TO BECOME A RIGHTDOER

It's not an appealing prospect to give a gift to someone who already took something precious from us, especially when they won't offer any gestures of contrition—or only inadequate, defensive, or half-hearted gestures. We feel like they owe us something, and we want to collect. Without admission, apology, contrition, responsibility, reparations, promises of reform, or at least guarantees of sincerity on the part of the wrongdoer, it's tough to forgive. So we wait for the wrongdoer to do something right for a change: make amends, grovel. We wait for the wrongdoer to apologize in the right way, with sufficient remorse, frequently enough, directly enough, using the right words and facial expressions. We wait for the offender to promise never to do it again. We wait for the offender to ask for forgiveness.

How long should we wait?

Some of us wait forever, believing that we can't forgive, or shouldn't, without an apology or any number of other hurdles we erect between ourselves and forgiveness. In that way, we stay trapped in our own pain.

"He makes it very hard to forgive," people tell me.

"It's hard when there's no remorse and a slick attorney."

"If only he would admit it. . . ."

Caryl Rivers, a professor of journalism at Boston University, cannot forgive the Roman Catholic priest who molested her brother Hugh when he was a child. Years later, Hugh committed suicide. "If the priest would give some sign of understanding at a moral level the chaos and terror he created, and make some attempt to atone for it, I could probably forgive him," says Rivers. "If a person like that decided to devote his time to meeting with families, and work with other men who were abusers, that certainly would demonstrate a commitment and genuine contrition."

Megan, the mother of a teenage victim of a hit-and-run accident, says, "How does one forgive someone who leaves your child lying in the street bleeding like some kind of animal?" Her only child, a sixteen-year-old boy, was bicycling along the shoulder of a Texas road in December 1995 when he was hit by a van. The driver was never caught.

Megan arrived at the hospital in time to kiss her son on the forehead and tell him she loved him before he was rushed into surgery. "They said if he lived he would lose his right leg. I didn't care about a leg. I just wanted them to save my son. But they couldn't. He had lost too much blood, and he died in surgery."

A single mother, Megan had been planning a private Christmas celebration with her son, who was her only family. Instead, she "ended up putting a small Christmas tree at the cemetery," she recalls. Then she "totally fell apart" and tried to kill herself.

More than three years later, she is remarried and grateful that her suicide attempt failed. But she feels unable to forgive. If the driver had stopped to help her son, "I most likely would have forgiven him that night," says Megan. "As long as the driver stays on the run, I can't forgive him, for he shows no signs of remorse. If he is ever caught, or ever turns himself in, then with Jesus's help I will work on forgiveness, as our Lord commands us to."

Asked to define forgiveness, Megan says, "A lot of people think that forgiveness means overlooking what the driver did and not wanting him to go to jail for it, but that's not what it means to me. He took a life, and he deserves to go to jail. To me forgiveness means that I could finally let go of the bitterness which I feel inside of myself for this person." Megan longs for closure, but without the driver's confession and remorse, she remains in limbo, unable to lift the heavy weight from her soul.

WE ASSOCIATE FORGIVENESS WITH CONDONING THE BEHAVIOR

The belief that most often interferes with forgiveness is this: To forgive is to condone. This is faulty logic: If you didn't find fault with someone's behavior, forgiveness would be moot. Of course, the behavior was wrong, stupid, insensitive, hurtful, criminal, whatever; that's why the possibility of forgiveness arises. But many of us withhold forgiveness as a way to express condemnation.

Sue, an associate professor in the college of education at an East Coast university, says her father was psychologically abusive to his children and physically violent with his wife. "Many times in my childhood, I would be lying in bed in utter terror as I would hear him screaming at my mother, crashing and banging. The next morning, my mother would say her bruises were because she fell against a wall." A hunter, her father kept guns in a corner right inside the front door. Sue would plan escape routes in case he started shooting everyone in the house. Both parents drank. When her mother fought back, her father's violence would escalate.

When her father died many years later, Sue had been having little contact with him for some time. Since then, through her own therapy, education, maturity, and Alcoholics Anonymous, Sue has become less bitter and angry. But to forgive her father in the absence of his taking responsibility for his behavior, she believes, would be "to say that he was okay. That's not the case."

WOMEN HAVE BEEN EXPECTED TO FORGIVE AND FORGET

Some women are wary of forgiveness, having been told too many times that they should forgive a man for various offenses, personal and political. "Forgive him" in this context tends to mean: Keep quiet, stop complaining, and let him off the hook.

A thirty-two-year-old rape victim named Nancy tells me she felt "a tremendous pressure to say that it's okay now, that it's over, and that I forgive him." But "it wasn't okay, so there's no way I forgive him."

Among professionals working with victimized women, "forgiveness is a loaded, controversial term," reports Cordelia Anderson, a violence prevention professional from Minneapolis. "People get so upset when they hear the word. They get very nervous about the victim being burdened with an unfair expectation. Victims should not be expected to forgive."

When Suzanne Freedman, coauthor of an article called "Forgiveness as an Intervention Goal with Incest Survivors," approached a rape crisis center in Madison, Wisconsin, to discuss a potential collaboration with them, "they did not want to have anything to do with me," she recalls. "Their philosophy is that they don't trust rapists, and they don't want to give them another chance. They're afraid of putting women back in a dangerous situation, and the prospect of forgiveness seems to represent that to them."

To compound women's ambivalence, women who do forgive men are often seen as fools. The subject of apology and forgiveness between men and women usually arises in this way: A story is told that a man beat a woman, or had an affair, then begged for forgiveness. When the storyteller goes on to say that the woman forgave him and "took him back," listeners react with confusion and anger. "She should not have forgiven him," they often say, or, "She was crazy to forgive him." These listeners typically do not forgive the man for his aggressive behavior. But neither do they forgive the woman for her seemingly foolish behavior. Along with the woman, forgiveness itself is portrayed as foolish.

WE'RE CYNICAL

A *Wall Street Journal* cartoon shows a group of people sitting around a conference table. One is saying, "It worked. We expressed remorse, asked for forgiveness, and sales are up 60 percent."

No wonder people are cynical about public pleas for forgiveness. We live in the age of apology, when you can hardly open a newspaper without reading about some politician or business leader or sports star apologizing for something—and wanting something in return. In June 1997, Mike Tyson apologized "to the world" for having "snapped in the ring" during a bout with Evander Holyfield. Without specifically admitting that he had bitten Holyfield's ear, he said, "I only ask that you forgive me as you have forgiven others in professional sports." He justified his behavior by describing it as part of a trend: "You have seen it in basketball with fist fights on the floor and in baseball with riots in the field and even spitting in the face of an official."

Apologies often look like this: They're accompanied by minimalizations ("if anyone was offended") and rationalizations ("I didn't mean it," "I snapped," "I'll get counseling," "others have also acted badly and you forgave them"). For good reason, people view these apologies with suspicion. Even sports fans have responded cynically to the recent pattern of crimes, apologies, and "second chances" for athletes who seem more interested in rehabilitating their careers than getting clear with the public or with God. Their apologies seem designed not to make amends but to make money. "Where there is big money, there is big forgiveness," explains Ferdie Pacheco, Muhammad Ali's former physician.[7]

WE BELIEVE WE SHOULD NOT FORGIVE IN CERTAIN CIRCUMSTANCES

Many of us have deep-seated beliefs about what's forgivable and what's unforgivable, about who should forgive whom, and how. Some of these come from religious teachings; some are harder to trace. One of these beliefs surfaced after a woman named Anita had a big fight with her brother, Rodney. Rodney has a history of drug abuse, has never kept a job for long, and lives with their parents, who are in their seventies. One day,

Anita searched Rodney's room, then confronted him about his storing illegal drugs there. Rodney exploded in a rage, cursed at her, and shoved her against a wall. Anita called the police.

Months later, Anita wrote Rodney a letter, apologizing for looking through his room. She added that she was still angry about his physical assault but recommended that they both "let bygones be bygones" for the sake of their parents, who were suffering because of the siblings' ongoing dispute.

Anita asked her husband to take the letter to their mailbox, offering him permission to read it along the way. After reading it, the husband refused to place it in the mailbox. "Why are you apologizing?" asked the husband. "Sure, you searched his room, but he threw you against a wall. Whoever is *more* wrong has to apologize first."

Is that true? When did the husband decide that whoever is more wrong has to apologize first? How many apologies have been thwarted because of that belief, or others?

"Forgiveness to the injured doth belong," said the English poet John Dryden. Jewish doctrine has formalized this, holding that only victims can forgive. The families of murder victims, then, cannot forgive. Nor can anyone forgive for the Holocaust, because the slain millions cannot speak for themselves. I've talked to some Gentiles who believe this too: that only victims can forgive. For some family members and friends of murder victims, this prohibition probably comes as a relief: There's no need to try to forgive. But for others, especially those who believe the murder victim would have wanted them to forgive, this belief may interfere with their desire to reopen their hearts, or regain an appreciation for life, or regain a sense of hope and compassion.

Other people's beliefs can also interfere. If you don't forgive, some may criticize you for hanging on to a grudge. If you do, you can be seen as weak. One man I interviewed later rescinded permission to use his name because he felt too exposed and vulnerable, he said. As he had begun to tell people about the process of forgiving his daughter's murderer, he had been unexpectedly assaulted by their belief that he was wrong to do so.

Some believe it's impossible to forgive. Some believe it's arrogant. Some believe only God can or should forgive for certain things. We must wait until the other person asks for forgiveness, some say. Or we shouldn't forgive incorrigible or unrepentant people.

Such beliefs get in the way of forgiveness. They become reasons not to forgive, explanations for nonforgiveness, justifications for clinging to grudges for years and years and years.

Often, people don't forgive because of a combination of these factors. Lynn, for instance, a young college graduate, explained to me in an e-mail that she will not forgive her stepfather because it would seem to condone his behavior, because she resents the church doctrine that tells her to forgive, because she disagrees with patriarchal teachings that tell women to forgive men, and because not forgiving feels more powerful.

"I was a victim of child abuse for nine years," she wrote. "It was not one event but a series of beatings that led to my hatred. He would hit us in places where people would not look. He liked sitting on us and choking us until we could not breathe so we could not scream anymore. I have several brothers that he treated the same way.

"In his eyes, the justification for the abuse was disobedience. The family was Mormon. He was the head of the household, and we were expected to obey without question. Children were to be seen and not heard. My problem was I questioned everything from the process of dying to why we could not watch TV on Sundays. I would question the gender of God. I was the smartest of the kids at home, and that threatened him. Whenever he could not find an answer, he would get mad.

"I am expected to forgive him and not talk about what happened. Have you heard the parable about the elephant being in a family's house and no one ever talking about it? That is my family. We never discuss it. I hate looking at him. I hate his eyes, his hands, his teeth. I used to do things just to get him going because I loved to see him lose control. It gave me a certain sense of power.

"The church says that I must forgive. I must turn the other cheek. I left the church. They condoned what he did. I have gained strength from not forgiving him. The hatred that I feel for him has helped me defend my brother against the same abuse. The hatred helped me move out when I was sixteen. The strength and power I get from not forgiving him has helped me put myself through school totally on my own.

"My forgiveness would only help my mother find justification in watching him beat her children. I am not finished grieving over the wounds he inflicted on me. I am going to be angry and unforgiving because I think women are expected to internalize the wrongs that have been inflicted on them and turn the other cheek. They are expected to be passive and take it. I am active, and I am still pissed."

She concluded her e-mail with this observation: "Wow, that brought up some stuff!"

Yes, questions about potential forgiveness "bring up some stuff": stories, memories, rage, resistance. Despite all the headaches and heartaches and hatred, it's easier not to even consider forgiveness. It brings up less stuff. Forgiveness means venturing into the unknown, and people tend to prefer the familiar. Forgiveness requires relinquishing the victim status, with all its attention, sympathy, righteousness, moral superiority, and energizing anger. Forgiveness means letting go of a certain kind of attachment to the perpetrator. Forgiveness hurts, too, because to forgive means to remember, and that often entails reexperiencing the hurt associated with the past.

Those of us who do not want to forgive (and any of us, at various times, could be included in that number) can find plenty of reasons not to, even more than I've listed here. A more worthwhile project would be to ask: Why forgive?

Chapter 3

WHY FORGIVE?

On my Power Macintosh, an "About This Computer" file charts how much memory is being used by various programs. One night, in a dream, I saw a similar chart for my "human system." It showed how much memory I'm consuming by not forgiving various friends and relatives. After I forgave someone, they no longer "drained the system" of memory and space.

How much energy, memory, and power are any of us wasting by hating so-and-so, resenting so-and-so, retelling stories about the despicable atrocities committed by so-and-so? To what uses might this space be put if it were not filled with unresolved pain?

A poem I wrote in my twenties and unearthed while writing this book led me to an answer to those questions. Entitled "Conversation Between a Woman and the Man Who Raped Her," the poem was inspired by a friend's story. At age twelve, a stranger raped her. She became pregnant and traveled to Mexico for an abortion.

In the poem, the rapist explains why she should forgive him. This part was pure fiction. I don't know where it came from. I wasn't thinking about Bruce at that time. I wasn't in touch with my rage or my need to forgive. Years later, while dealing with Bruce and pondering the question *Why forgive?* I was surprised to dig up this dusty poem. There, repeated for emphasis in the last stanza, was the answer I was looking for: because "then you will have an open heart." I'd known it all along. Maybe we all do.

CONVERSATION BETWEEN A WOMAN AND THE MAN WHO RAPED HER

SHE SAYS
> *I told you to stop*
> *I told you it hurt*
> *I said, "You're hurting me"*
> *I said, "Don't you understand you're hurting me?"*

HE SAYS
> *You must have been only twelve*
> *I was thirty-six, in unbearable pain.*
> *I didn't stop*
> *to notice your youth, your bruised*
> *skin, the color of your hair, was incapable*
> *of caring, don't you see?*
> *Did you look at my face?*
> *Did you see a happy man?*

SHE SAYS
> *I have my own pain.*
> *I have a clenched fist where my heart belongs*
> *Instead of a heart: a clenched fist.*

HE SAYS
> *And you have your own task, more difficult than anger or fear.*

SHE SAYS
> *Why should I forgive you?*

HE SAYS

> *If you forgive, your heart will open*
> *Then you will have an open heart.*
> *If you forgive, your heart will open*
> *Then you will have an open heart.*

The poem was never published. Maybe it's not a very good poem. But I'm not applying for a poetry prize here. I'm sharing the poem just to make this point: I believe the "he" in the poem is right about the primary reason to forgive—because then you will have an open heart.

It's as practical as that. Do you want your life to become one huge catalog of grievances? Do you want to remain forever obsessed with the people who hurt you? Do you want to lust primarily for revenge?

Not forgiving is toxic. Grudges and grievances pollute your mind, body, and relationships. Saint Thomas Aquinas said: "If you hate someone, your sword must first pierce your own soul." So when asking, *Why forgive?* you must also ask, *What are the consequences of not forgiving? What effect will nonforgiveness have on me?*

Long the exclusive province of theology, forgiveness has now caught the attention of researchers in medicine and psychology, who are documenting the connection between hating someone and "piercing one's own soul." In their groundbreaking research in the seventies, Dr. O. Carl Simonton and his colleagues concluded that emotional states affect people's susceptibility to illness and that the following four characteristics are found disproportionately among people with cancer:

- A poor self-image

- An inadequate ability to form and sustain long-term relationships

- A tendency toward self-pity

- "A tendency to hold resentment and a sustained inability to forgive."[1]

Simonton, a radiation oncologist, says that lack of forgiveness contributes to emotional distress, which is the "number one risk factor for disease in the developed world. It's surprising how rapid relief of physical symptoms can often be found through emotional healing."

Robert Enright has been researching forgiveness since 1985. A professor of educational psychology at the University of Wisconsin, Enright helped generate interest in forgiveness with a research program at the university and with the establishment in 1995 of the International Forgiveness Institute. "Those who carry around hatred and anger make themselves ill. Those who learn to forgive can find wellness," he says.

He summarizes the research from five different studies: "Those who learn to forgive improve their physical health, lower anxiety, lower psychological depression, lower anger, increase a sense of well-being, increase self-esteem, and increase hope." In a long-term intervention with female incest survivors, for example, forgiving those who had assaulted them enabled the women to become more hopeful, improved their self-esteem, and helped them to experience less anxiety and depression.[2] Forgiveness therapy for elderly women and college students has proven effective in reducing depression and anxiety and in raising self-esteem.[3] In one study of college students who perceived themselves to be "parentally love-deprived," participation in forgiveness workshops decreased their anxiety and increased their positive attitudes toward their parents.[4] In another study, men who self-identified as having been hurt by their partner's abortion were treated with therapy that focused on forgiveness. Compared to a control group, the forgiveness group experienced less anger, anxiety, and grief.[5]

Psychologists and psychiatrists have also begun noting reductions in anger, depression, and anxiety in patients who forgive their offenders.[6] Richard Fitzgibbons, a Philadelphia psychiatrist who helped introduce forgiveness to the mental health field, sees among his forgiving patients "an enhanced ability to trust, a freedom from subtle control of individuals and events from the past, and increased feelings of love."

Forgiveness research is controversial because people associate it with religion and because some scientists criticize it as a "soft" area of research. But, Enright says, "our findings have been a lot stronger than expected and have withstood the test of time. Usually in the social sciences, our results are quite modest and mixed. I figured it would make a difference, but I'm surprised at how powerful forgiveness actually is for emotional healing."

Jackie Pflug intuitively understood the healing power of forgiveness. Pflug was a passenger on the Egyptian Air jet that was en route from

Athens to Cairo when Palestinian terrorists forced it to land in Malta. Fifty-one people aboard that airliner died, some shot at point-blank range and dumped onto the runway, others in a fire that started when Egyptian commandos stormed the plane. The killings began after the terrorists collected passports and announced that unless their demands were met, they would shoot all the Israelis, then the Americans. Pflug, an American, watched as the first Israeli passenger was shot in the head and then dumped on the runway. When she moved, the hijacker shot her again until she stopped moving. The executions continued, one every fifteen minutes.

When Pflug was brought to the front of the plane and shot, she felt her brain explode. "I knew that I had been shot, and I knew that my body was hitting the staircase, but . . . it felt like I was just floating on air," Pflug said.

Thinking she was dead, she expected to open her eyes and see heaven. Instead she saw the runway. "That's when I closed my eyes and I started to play dead. I remembered the Israeli woman who was shot just hours before, and every time she moved, she got shot. So I lay there perfectly still."

Pflug survived, but with brain damage. Her vision, memory, and ability to speak were severely impaired. She lost her teaching job.

After ten years of grief, therapy, and physical rehabilitation, she testified against the man who had shot her, Omar Mohammed Ali Rezaq. His lawyer argued that he should be forgiven because he grew up in poverty, surrounded by violence; because he was indoctrinated from an early age to hate Israelis and Americans; and because he regretted his actions. Nevertheless, he was convicted of hijacking and murder and sentenced to life in prison with the recommendation that he never be granted parole.

National Public Radio reporter Daniel Zwerdling asked Pflug recently "whether, anywhere inside you, you feel like you can, in some way, forgive him."

"Oh, there's no doubt that I have already forgiven him," Pflug responded. "I did it because I noticed in the first two years my body was starting to give me seizures. I was having these incredible headaches. The doctors didn't know where the pain was coming from. But I did." The pain was coming from "all the hatred and bitterness I was storing up inside for this man. So I started to learn how to forgive and I did it for myself."[7]

In 1998 the John Templeton Foundation contributed almost $5 million to twenty-nine new projects in forgiveness research related to both physical and mental health. The response to its call for proposals was so overwhelming that the foundation plans to spearhead a fund-raising campaign to raise another $5 million to support the work it rejected in the first round of applications. Topics of study include the role of forgiveness with trauma patients, terminally ill patients, newlyweds, and marriages damaged by affairs. Researchers will also study political reconciliation in Northern Ireland, South Africa, and Rwanda.[8]

One grant recipient is Frederic Luskin, director of the Stanford Forgiveness Project at the Stanford Center for Research and Disease Prevention. Luskin, who became interested in the field when he noticed his own inability to forgive a friend's betrayal, has found that forgiving protects against disease and improves emotional health. People who forgive become less angry and more optimistic. In one experiment, fifty-five volunteers were asked to think of someone they had not forgiven for something and to rate their level of hurt on a scale of 1 to 10. Most ranked their hurt at 8, with 10 being the most hurt. After undergoing forgiveness training, which involved meditation and cognitive therapy, most ranked the hurt at about 3. Ten weeks later, the level stayed the same. "You can train people to forgive quickly," he reports.

Luskin is currently studying gender differences in forgiveness, hypothesizing that men don't mind feeling uncomfortable about relationships and hence are less driven to forgive. Forgiveness is "a woman word," he says.

Luskin believes that letting go of grudges can have broad consequences. "Not only can we teach you to forgive a particular person who has hurt you, but through that process you can learn to generally become a less angry, less easily insulted soul. You will probably build better relationships."

Bud Welch, the father of a twenty-three-year-old victim of the Oklahoma City bombing, also knows the healing power of forgiveness. He says of Timothy McVeigh, "I haven't forgiven him yet," but adds, "It's something I know I need to do before I die. It's something you need to do for your own well-being. You don't need to force yourself, but you need to start dealing with things. If not, you're very bitter."

In *Mr. Ives' Christmas,* a lovely novel by Oscar Hijuelos, Mr. Ives expresses the same motivation—exorcising his own bitterness—when attempting to forgive the boy who murdered his son. Mr. Ives's teenage son was killed by another teenage boy in a senseless street shooting, and the father discovers over time that "the years of longing and of missing his son, without being able to forget or forgive, had taken their toll on him. He'd turned into stone. It had been difficult to show affection to his own wife."

Mr. Ives begins to spend time with the killer's grandmother, who is also distraught about the crime, and "as the years went by, Ives and the grandmother were getting along to the point where on several occasions, in the name of doing the 'Christian' thing, he picked her up in a taxi and took her to support-group meetings . . . for victims of crimes and their families." Mr. Ives heard "hundreds of stories of heartache and tragedy, and concluded that the only way to deal with suffering was to trust in God and cling to the path of righteousness, and this he did." He had doubts "but pushed onward with the conviction that sooner or later there would be some kind of payoff, some sense that goodness, in and of itself, was its own reward."

At one of these meetings, the grandmother weeps and shows the group photos of her grandson before and after the murders. "The good part of him is asleep, that's all," she says. "He's still good inside; that part must be awakened." This comment inspires Mr. Ives to "rehabilitate her grandson, for in helping him, he would bring some kind of relief to the grandmother and perhaps to himself."

To the bewilderment of his wife and friends, Mr. Ives begins corresponding with his son's murderer in prison. He mails the young criminal care packages: letters, a Bible, food, comics, and a radio. He encourages him to enroll in high school equivalency classes. Mr. Ives explains his generosity: "For a long time, I felt so bitter toward this young man that it was poisoning me inside, so I had to do something to get the poison out of myself."[9]

This book is beautiful in part because of its emotional honesty. Forgiveness is usually a long process that can include hatred, a desire for revenge, then a gradual awareness that these responses, when prolonged, can be toxic. It's often at that point—when people realize that their accumulated rage is making them mentally or physically ill—that they consider the forgiveness option.

In a real-life version of *Mr. Ives' Christmas,* Azim Khamisa forgave the fourteen-year-old boy, Tony Hicks, who murdered his son. Guided by a different faith—Islamic Ismaili—Khamisa developed a friendship with the young murderer's grandfather, Ples Felix, and the two of them decided to "think along the lines of love, forgiveness, and compassion, instead of following the path of blame, hatred, and anger." In his book, *Azim's Bardo,* Khamisa quotes from the Qur'anic Ayat:

> . . . *remember God's favor on you*
> *For ye were enemies*
> *and He joined your hearts*
> *In love, so that by His grace*
> *Ye became brethren.*

He notes that hatred "can corrode our insides like a virulent acid," and he thanks God that he has chosen the path of forgiveness instead.[10]

"We are who we are because of the stories we tell ourselves about ourselves," Tom Spanbauer wrote in *The Man Who Fell in Love with the Moon.*[11] In the process of healing, forgivers start telling themselves different stories. The perpetrator's leading role shrinks to a less important part. The bitter obsession—with the offense, or with the offender, or with the hope for revenge, reparations, or reconciliation—fades. The victim is released from "a life of perpetual connection to the offense," the family therapists Wes Crenshaw and Greg Tangari have observed.[12]

At age sixteen, Debbie Morris was abducted for two days and raped by the man made famous by the movie *Dead Man Walking* (which was only loosely based on Morris's story). Robert Willie and his accomplice, Joseph Vaccaro, never showed remorse—neither for raping Morris nor for stabbing her boyfriend and leaving him for dead (he survived), nor for killing another woman in a previous abduction.

Fifteen years later, Morris wrote her own book, *Forgiving the Dead Man Walking.* In response to those who asked how she could forgive

Willie, Morris wrote, "The refusal to forgive him always meant that I held onto all my Robert Willie–related stuff—my pain, my shame, my self-pity. That's what I gave up in forgiving him. And it wasn't until I did that real healing could even begin."

One motivation for Morris was to avoid the ugly bitterness that she saw consuming the parents of the murdered girl. These parents called Morris repeatedly, ostensibly to see how she was doing but also to vent their own fury at Willie. "Seeing the effects of their abiding anger and hatred . . . helped convince me I needed to let go of those feelings myself. As weird as this may seem, I doubt I would ever have tried to forgive Robert Willie if it hadn't been for my unsettling exposure to such an all-consuming bitterness."[13]

For Morris, as for many forgivers, opening one door of her heart led to opening others. After she forgave Willie, she forgave her mother (for drinking and mismanaging their money when she was a child, and for seeming to not care where she was the night she was abducted); God (for allowing the abduction to happen); Robert Willie's mother (for testifying falsely in court); and Sister Helen Prejean (for offering spiritual guidance to Robert Willie but never contacting Morris).

Forgivers reclaim control of their lives. "It's so much more empowering than sitting around feeling wronged," says a woman who forgave her husband after their divorce. Forgivers become strong enough to heal, big enough to notice who else is also hurting, energetic enough to reach out and extend themselves to others. Forgivers release themselves from the victim identity, from forever being tied to the offender. Rather than staying defeated, they start thinking of themselves as powerful, effective, creative.

Just as there are physical and emotional benefits to forgiving, there are spiritual benefits as well. Eleanor, the jazz musician's widow, says that forgiveness allowed her to "make room for God." Her husband was addicted to alcohol and other drugs. "When he was sober, he was a gentle, sweet, nonviolent man," says Eleanor. "But when he was drunk, he was a tremendously scary person. He was extremely violent with me, with his children, and with his dog, whom he loved and adored."

Eleanor consciously practiced forgiveness throughout the thirty-two-year marriage, something she found "tremendously difficult" because she "didn't want to encourage further abuse," she says. "Unforgivable things happen," but even then "you don't have to get revenge or teach someone a lesson. You can practice letting go and letting God, as we say in Al-Anon."

When forgiveness is possible, "it's a giving gesture to yourself, not allowing yourself to be hung up on previous resentments. Once you let go of various forms of personal, emotional, and sometimes physical injury, then you make room for all sorts of positive emotions. You make room for God, in a sense. You make room for solutions. If you're stuck on problems, which resentments undoubtedly are, there's no place in your heart for goodness, solutions, sharing, caring. It's taken a while for me, but I have come to understand that forgiveness is necessary for my own sanity."

With Peter and Linda Biehl, faith played a different role. Rather than forgiveness making room for God, God made room for forgiveness. Linda had just returned home from a back-to-school shopping trip with her son when one of her daughters called, informing her that Amy, another daughter, had been killed by a South African mob.

After that, the phone kept ringing. The U.S. ambassador called, reporters called, relatives and friends called. Everyone offered condolences, then waited to hear Linda's response—which was not, as many expected, rage. She was shocked and devastated, like any mother whose beloved child has been killed. But, clutching the phone, Linda Biehl paced around her southern California kitchen saying over and over, "Forgive them, Father, for they know not what they've done."

Amy Biehl, a twenty-six-year-old American Fulbright scholar, had been a high school valedictorian, a Stanford diver, and an ultra-marathoner. She was working in South Africa in 1993, helping with voter registration for the nation's first all-races election in 1994, when she was killed by a mob of between fifty and two hundred men. As well as she could, Amy had prepared her parents for the day of her death, telling them that the frustrated and angry black South African youth shouldn't be blamed for their violence since they were "only doing what has been done to them by generations of white oppressors."

A lifetime of Christian practice and teaching also prepared Linda and Peter Biehl for that day. "We grew up in churches, we raised four children in Presbyterian churches, we taught Sunday school, we taught Christian ethics, so we'd be terrible heretics if we couldn't take the position that Linda took within minutes," says Peter Biehl, a strategic business consultant.

The South African criminal justice system convicted four of the young men of murder and public violence and sentenced them to eighteen years of hard labor in prison. The men then applied for amnesty under the Truth and Reconciliation Commission guidelines, which stipulated that the applicants had to confess, show that the crime was politically motivated, and apologize to the victim or family.

Linda and Peter traveled to South Africa for the hearing and, by happenstance, encountered the four murderers in the hallway outside the hearing room. "I was within inches of my daughter's killers, and somehow I was in control of my emotions," recalls Peter. "In retrospect, I know Amy's hand was on my shoulder at that moment. Linda has said she didn't feel anger, only a sort of profound sadness, a void."

Peter says that he and Linda "had more feeling for the parents of the men. I believe the experience must have been more difficult for them than for us. One left the courtroom when her son confessed to stabbing Amy in the heart."

In their own statement to the commission, Peter and Linda Biehl said they would not stand in the way of amnesty being granted to the men who had murdered their daughter. Amy would have supported this process, they said.

All four men were granted amnesty and released unconditionally. Peter now says that he and Linda harbor "no grudge, no desire for revenge. We sincerely hope that the families and communities will gather around them and give them the support necessary to live productive lives in a nonviolent atmosphere. We hope they grow up well. We're not going to waste any time worrying about it, or regretting that they have been given a second chance."

For the Biehls, forgiveness means freedom. "We feel absolutely, completely liberated, rather than exercising the extreme energy taken for revenge," says Peter.

They sound like saints. It's almost inconceivable for the parents of a murdered child to go directly to forgiveness without wading, or nearly drowning, in rage along the way. Yet as I talk with Peter five years after the killing, his forgiveness sounds genuine. He and Linda still grieve the loss of Amy, he says, "and don't want closure on her life," but there is a lightness in Peter's voice, and easy laughter.

Peter also asks, "Who are we to dispense forgiveness? We're just two people. It's between a person and his God. All we can say is we harbor no grudge, no desire for reparations. And we're free. We sleep very well at night."

The more you forgive, the more virtuous you feel. Not better than the wrongdoer, but better than before, when you were merely a passive victim of fate. As a forgiver, you add goodness to the world and can in turn enjoy that feeling of generosity. In that state of mind, you're likely to feel not only healthier but also more forgiving of other human mistakes, including your own.

Beyond the personal, individual benefits of forgiveness are the relational benefits: to marriages, families, communities, nations. Some marriage counselors say forgiveness is the single most important ingredient in a healthy marriage. I agree: We need to forgive our partners repeatedly, in response to each slight or disappointment or failure. We also need to receive our partner's forgiveness. In a good relationship, we bask in the fact of that forgiveness, sometimes expressed only in smiles and kind gestures. The word *forgive* need never be spoken. But I think many of us need this almost daily goodwill in order to continue loving ourselves and each other.

Forgiveness can also spread compassion throughout families and communities. A parent's forgiving behavior teaches a child to forgive herself, and eventually to forgive her own children, who can then raise children of their own in a forgiving climate. A teacher's forgiveness of her students, and of herself, can set an example, showing the whole class what's possible. Azim Khamisa chose to institutionalize his goodwill by establishing a foundation in honor of his murdered son; it's dedicated to teaching nonviolence to children. He chose to "focus on future violence prevention, not past violence punishment," he says. He has also invited his son's murderer to come work at the Tariq Khamisa Foundation when he is released from prison.

One of the most remarkable things about forgiveness is that it encourages people to change their behavior. This is counterintuitive: We tend to think that we should forgive only after people change, indeed, that we should withhold forgiveness until they change. But I don't think it works that way.

I think forgiveness implicitly gives wrongdoers permission to forgive themselves, thus decreasing the number of self-hating people in the world—as well as the likelihood that guilt, shame, and self-loathing will be vented on some other victim. The generosity of the forgiver enables the wrongdoer to see herself in a better light, thus raising the probability that she will behave better in the future. Released from shame, that person becomes free to spread more goodwill through the community.

Sister Helen Prejean raises this issue in her book *Dead Man Walking:* "What if criminals had at some point in their lives been forgiven?" We don't know the answer to that question, but it's reasonable to think that forgiveness enriches the lives of those who receive it—major offenders as well as minor transgressors. It's also reasonable to think that forgiveness permits people to start thinking of themselves in new ways. When Sister Prejean offers forgiveness to one of the death row inmates she counsels, he looks shocked. "That's the first time anyone ever said that to me," he tells her.[14] Clearly, it made an impression.

Father Lawrence Martin Jenco saw this dynamic in effect when he forgave his captors—unconditionally—before they had even released him. A former program director for Catholic Relief Services in Beirut, Lebanon, Jenco was kidnapped by Shiite Muslims and kept in a series of makeshift prisons for 564 days. Despite beatings, starvation, isolation, mental cruelty, and unsanitary conditions, the priest could write these words to his family at Christmas 1991:

> Dear brothers and sisters,
> If I am to die, I hope that I would die with the words of Jesus on my lips: "Father, forgive them; for they do not know what they are doing." Please do not hate them. . . .
>
> *Much love, Larry*[15]

Several months later, while still captive, he learned that his captors had kept the letter, never mailing it. One of these men read Jenco's own words back to him, "not because he wanted me to know it had not been sent; rather he used its words to ask for forgiveness," explains Jenco, who granted the request.

Toward the end of Jenco's captivity, a particularly brutal captor named Sayeed asked Jenco's forgiveness for the beatings he had inflicted on him. "I was called to forgive, to let go of revenge, retaliation, and vindictiveness," writes Jenco in *Bound to Forgive*. "And I was challenged to forgive him unconditionally. I could not forgive him on the condition that he change his behavior to conform to my wishes and values. I had no control over his response." Jenco did forgive Sayeed. He then proceeded to asks his captor's forgiveness (and God's) for the hatred, anger, and revenge he had felt toward him.[16]

Like the Biehls, Jenco sounds like a saint. And like the Biehls, Jenco had a lifetime of Christian teaching to guide him. But even if such drastic, unconditional forgiveness feels out of reach for most people, it's instructive. Jenco's forgiveness gave these kidnappers permission to change. Apparently, it was because they read his letter that they humbled themselves and asked for his forgiveness. If Jenco had not written that he had forgiven them, they might never have reached that place.

It seems to me that if you forgive someone, that person usually senses it and feels less uncomfortable around you, even if you never discuss it. They probably are able to see you without being haunted by memories of the awful thing they did to you. Your presence no longer reminds them of their own feelings and failings. And they probably stop blaming you for sparking their own guilt. Even if your forgiveness does not always have a perceptible impact—some people are too scared and scarred to change—they might be capable of changing in the future. In any case, you're free from bitterness, vengefulness, anger, hatred.

I experimented with this sort of preemptive forgiveness with a colleague who betrayed my trust. She broke a verbal contract, and the demise of our deal cost me about $1,000 in travel costs and more than two weeks' time. It also cost me a lot of headaches as I waited for her to make good on her word and argued with her about it, to no avail.

Yet this is someone whom I respect in other ways and see at professional gatherings once or twice a year. I chose not to hold on to my anger about her betrayal. Without ever specifically saying it, I forgave her. The next time I saw her, I reached out to her, complimenting her on a recent success. I followed that with a personal note congratulating her on another achievement, the way I might with any colleague. These actions let her know that she didn't need to fear my wrath. She became relaxed in my company, unguarded and friendly. She was forgiven, and "hence she has shown great love."

That phrase comes to mind because of a biblical passage (Luke 7:36–50) in which Jesus explains that people become more loving *after* they are forgiven. Referring to a "sinner" who has been forgiven for her sins, Jesus says, "Therefore, I tell you, her sins, which were many, have been forgiven; hence she has shown great love."[17]

"Hence" means "for this reason," or "therefore," or "from this source," or "from this time forward." Jesus seems to be saying that ever since she was forgiven, the sinner has shown great love. The following line supports that: "But the one to whom little is forgiven, loves little." In other words, if you aren't forgiven very often—like the death row inmates Helen Prejean works with—you won't love much. Forgiveness creates room for love.

Frederick A. DiBlasio, a professor of social work at the University of Maryland at Baltimore, believes that long-term counseling usually falters unless a patient *at the outset* forgives the offender. "You can still have hurt feelings," he says, "but the bottom line is, you choose not to harbor those resentments." Like other researchers, DiBlasio plans to test his hypothesis with a Templeton Foundation grant.[18]

"I need to have this conversation too," Bruce told me the first time I called him.

Now that I have taken a serious look at the ways I too crave forgiveness, I know what Bruce meant. Most of us want to be forgiven, for offenses large and small. This fact provides a final reason to forgive: We know what it's like to crave forgiveness. Remembering this makes it easier, and more important, to offer it to our fellow human beings. We all "need to have this conversation."

Your forgiveness may help other people heal, and it may even free them to think of themselves in a more positive way. Your forgiveness may make a contribution to family harmony, or community harmony, or even world peace. But here's the primary reason to forgive: When you forgive, you become human again, no longer "turned to stone." When you forgive, you no longer have "a clenched fist" where your heart belongs. You unburden your heart. Goodness is its own reward.

Part II

FIVE KEYS TO FORGIVENESS AND FREEDOM

Chapter 4

AWARENESS:
THE COURAGE TO INQUIRE

*F*orgiveness does not begin with clarity. It begins with pain. Few of us would explore forgiveness if it weren't for this pain, coupled with a desire to feel better and a willingness to risk more pain and uncertainty en route to freedom.

Pain leads to questions: *What happened? What were the consequences? Why am I still hurting? Who was responsible? Why did that person act as they did? Is there a way to feel better?*

In my case, it took a long time before I started asking myself: *What exactly happened between Bruce and me?* The question finally arose because, as a sportswriter, I was noticing a pattern among coaches and athletes that was similar to my experience. What they were doing did not look like "an affair" or "dating," though they sometimes camouflaged it with those words. It looked like exploitation. It made me wonder: *Was I exploited too? If so, what effect did that experience have on me?*

My adolescent relationship with Bruce had been characterized by playfulness and laughter; swimming meets and practices; basketball and badminton; earnest discussions about books, politics, and religion; skinny-dipping in the pool late at night; his hand on my thigh; his hand in my pants; my heart in my throat; my shame; my confusion; and my coping strategy: This must be love.

He treated me romantically, giving me gifts, including a poster with the then-popular Frederick S. Perls quote: "I did not come into this world to live up to your expectations, and you did not come into this world to live up to mine . . . but if by chance we find each other, it's beautiful."

I was in heaven—Bruce loved me!—and also in hell: I was immoral for having sex with a married man.

Even the poster was problematic. It was the first poem anyone had given me, and I was eager to hang it on my bedroom wall. But that too seemed shameful and scary: What if my parents asked where I got it? Would I get in trouble for receiving such a poster from my coach? My decision to hide both the poster and the truth from my parents led to even more shame.

Shortly after I turned sixteen, my father got a new job and we moved across the country; that move abruptly ended the abuse but also separated me from the only person with whom I could discuss this confusing relationship. For many years it didn't occur to me to blame him. It was less painful somehow to believe that I was an adulteress than to believe that the man I loved took advantage of me. Even when I read accounts of incest survivors and saw myself in their stories, I didn't come to terms with the fact that Bruce had betrayed me. I continued to tell people—and myself—that my first sexual relationship had been "an affair with a married man."

As recently as 1993, while drafting *The Stronger Women Get, the More Men Love Football,* I referred to Bruce as "my first lover," described "our affair," and titled the chapter "My Coach, My Lover." Only after a friend's gentle editing did I rename the chapter "My Coach Says He Loves Me" and change *lover* and *affair* to *molester* and *sexual abuse.*

I changed my language, and the way I thought about the relationship, because over time, as I reflected on my experience with Bruce, I realized that I had indeed been exploited. We were not peers. We were not lovers. He was an adult, and I was a minor, and he seduced me into having sex with him. Even the phrase "we had sex" no longer made sense. A more accurate description was "he did sex to me." I was in junior high when the sexual contact began. Over the course of three summers, with occasional winter rendezvous when I baby-sat his children, he performed various sexual acts on me. Though I did not resist, the sex was his idea, he initiated it, and for the most part I was passive, too nervous and naive to respond. Now I know that this is not what "lovers" do. It's not an "affair." It's not "having sex." Even if I had been sophisticated and aggressive, it still would have been sexual exploitation and statutory rape. At fourteen, fifteen, and sixteen, I was too innocent to understand that.

It took two decades before I comprehended that I had been molested and legally raped. This was not a welcome insight. While for some victims it might be a relief to realize they were not responsible for an illicit "affair," for me it was painful to come to terms with the fact that I had been victimized. I had never thought of myself as a victim and didn't relish it. I hadn't wanted to be molested. I'd wanted to be loved, and I preferred to think of it that way. Yet in order to even consider forgiving Bruce in some authentic and meaningful way, I had to begin with the facts.

In 1993 I called Bruce out of the blue, saying, "I want to ask you some questions." We hadn't spoken in almost twenty years.

I was calling for professional reasons, it seemed to me. I figured Bruce might be able to offer insights into the phenomenon of coach-athlete sex. I had been having trouble finding coaches to interview. They kept lying to me or slamming down the phone. I thought: *There's one man who can't lie to me, because I was there.* Maybe, out of some sense of obligation, Bruce would respond to my questions. Why had he molested me? What had he been thinking? How did he feel about the experience now? How many other girls had he molested? I was not consciously angry at the time, just curious.

"How did you feel about me then?" I asked.

He paused.

"Don't you remember?" I pressed, impatient.

"I'm searching," he said. "It wasn't the ordinary type thing. Was there feeling? Yes. Can I 100 percent identify that? No. Obviously, there was friendship. Obviously, there was a mutual attraction. Obviously, there was a terrific comfort and trust level. I enjoyed your company. There were discussions, there was laughter, there was sharing. Many things were good and meaningful. Do I say, it must have been love? There was probably a fear to express that."

I asked him how he felt about the experience now. He said that he thought about it almost daily, and that for twenty years he had suffered from a "self-inflicted flogging." He said he had "gone through a lot of things, even religiously, in terms of regret." He said, "It's a very crushing feeling to me to think that I've ever had any kind of negative impact on you. Crushing."

"You did," I said bluntly. I told him what a burden the sex and secrecy had been, how ashamed I had felt of my own "adulterous" behavior, how my trust had been broken.

"I'm so very sorry," he said.

Had he had sex with other girls? I wanted to know.

He admitted brief incidents with two of my friends but denied responsibility, saying angrily, "I was drunk!" He insisted that there had been no others. "I'm a different person," he said. "I've grown."

He also tried to dodge responsibility for our "affair," saying, at one point, "Okay, so we made a mistake."

"You made a mistake," I corrected him.

"Don't you think you had any responsibility?" he asked plaintively.

"No. I was a child," I said.

"Okay, you're right," he said. Then: "It wasn't forced. It wasn't drug-induced. I wasn't trying to get you to a state where you didn't have any inhibitions. It wasn't sexual harassment."

"It was statutory rape," I said.

He paused again. Then: "You don't know how badly, if I hurt you, that I want you not just to accept an apology from me but to forgive me."

Forgiveness often begins like this: with questions, with apologies, with an awkward, angry, defensive conversation between a victim and a perpetrator. It leads to glimpses of the truth.

Truth is what Bishop Desmond Tutu was seeking as he chaired the Truth and Reconciliation Commission's historic investigation into South Africa's apartheid era. When he uncovered the truth, it was difficult to stomach. "I have been overwhelmed by the depth of depravity and evil," he said. "I am devastated to hear police officers describe how they drugged the coffee of one of their captives, shot him behind the ear, and then set his body on fire. That is bad enough, but it is all made more appalling by the police describing how while this cremation was taking place, they had a barbecue, turning over two sets of meat, as it were."

The investigation revealed some more heartening facts as well. "There is also the other side," continued Tutu, "the story of the victims, the survivors who were made to suffer so grievously, yet despite this are ready to forgive. This magnanimity, this nobility of spirit, is quite breathtakingly unbelievable."

Not all the victims or survivors were ready to forgive, of course. Tutu noted that their reticence demonstrates "that forgiveness is not facile or cheap. It is a costly business that makes those who are willing to forgive even more extraordinary."

Dexter King began with that willingness to forgive, but he also needed facts. Martin Luther King's son was seven when his father was assassinated. James Earl Ray confessed and was sentenced to ninety-nine years in prison. What Dexter King remembers is that "my mother guided us spiritually not to hate the person who did it." Yet he too sought information, calling for a reopening of the investigation in the late 1990s, shortly before Ray died, explaining that he wasn't seeking "retributive justice" but wanted simply "to lay all the facts on the table," because facts are necessary for healing.

When a victim seeks information about the past, he might have hope for his own future, or hope for reconciliation with the perpetrator, or no hope, just anger, but he must bring some willingness to ask and talk and listen. The word *forgiveness* enters the conversation when the perpetrator says, "I'd like you to forgive me," or, "Please forgive me," or, "I hope you have forgiven me." The victim asserts that he has already forgiven, or says that he wants to forgive, or swears he'll never forgive. Regardless, the word *forgive* has appeared, dangling between them like a balloon. It has emerged as a possibility, however remote.

En route to forgiving the man who killed his daughter, Adam was asking many good questions. One of his first was, "What exactly happened to Billie Jo?"

Billie Jo was eighteen years old when a man sexually assaulted and killed her. The man was found guilty of rape, abduction, and murder and sentenced to life in prison.

With assistance from a professional mediator, Adam has visited his daughter's murderer in prison several times in the six years since the assault. Forgiveness was not on his mind when he initiated the meetings, Adam reports, "because that was not part of my consciousness. I would not have said, 'I'm in the midst of a forgiveness process.'" But in hindsight, he says, "I can see that I needed to be at a certain place in order to meet with that man. By the first time we met, I had already moved in that direction."

Adam's original agenda was threefold: to convey to the killer the murder's horrific impact on Adam's family; to obtain information about the crime; and "to understand what the man's life was like," both before and after the murder. "Who was this man," Adam wondered, "and what was happening to him as a result of this?"

The killer, a twenty-four-year-old who did not plead guilty at the trial, has not apologized directly to Adam. Yet over the course of the meetings, which are "intense," Adam says, he has seen in his daughter's murderer some things he can "respect and appreciate." The murderer "sees himself as making a contribution to the community, so to speak, where he's living. He's looking for some kind of meaning in his life. He has a significant relationship with his family."

Adam says that his "personal experience of forgiveness," which he describes as "a process, not an event," now includes "a lowering of anger, resentment, and hostility, being able to wish this man well, not wanting further harm to come to him or his family." He says he has "basically been able to see the humanity of this man, to appreciate his contributions, whatever they may be."

Nevertheless, he still feels enraged sometimes and wonders, "When is righteous rage necessary, and how much is needed? Might we, in a desperate search for forgiveness, harm ourselves by reducing the rage?"

A man of many questions, Adam is also asking himself, "To what degree is it helpful for me or for him if he becomes aware of my experience of forgiveness?" The word *forgive* has come up in Adam's meetings, but he has not informed the murderer of his own process in any detail. He wonders whether his offering of forgiveness could in any way undermine the legal system's "appropriate response" to the man's criminal acts. Might the man be released too soon if the parole board heard of Adam's forgiveness? "I'm still struggling with that," says Adam. "When are you enabling, when are you empowering, when are you rehabilitating?"

Adam's forgiveness is "highly unusual," according to the professional mediator who is working with him. "Most families, under those circumstances, do not forgive," he says. Indeed, some family members of other murder victims have criticized Adam for moving toward forgiveness with this killer. Remarkably open-minded, Adam wonders, "Why do some people find forgiveness offensive, and what can I learn from them?"

He also asks himself, "To what degree do I want to continue meeting with this man?" Throughout this process, Adam has not lost his faith. In fact, he feels blessed with "a feeling of grace." He has "not felt abandoned by God," he says. "Though I've certainly had some questions."

It takes courage to inquire: What happened? What else happened? Whose fault was it? Who was that person? It requires courage because you don't know at first what the answers will be, nor can you know where the path will lead, and whether it will include a sense of peace and resolution. You risk reexperiencing the pain of the original injury as you expose and cleanse the wound. You risk feeling overwhelmed by fury or grief as you remember what occurred, and how you felt about it then, and how you feel about it now.

"A psychologist told me that in order for me to heal, I have to let it all out," a teacher writes to me, explaining that she was abused by her parents but "never really dealt with it." She explains, "As a busy professional, I am afraid that if I let it unravel, I will lose my composure, my control, even my sanity, and that will affect everything I have worked so hard for."

I could not tell this woman not to worry. If you have contact with the person who hurt you, you risk hearing answers you don't want to hear, or don't agree with. You might be tricked or deceived or abused again; you might feel foolish. Even if you do not have contact with that person, you risk realizing that things were not as bad you had remembered them. Or that they were worse. Or that you were partially or wholly at fault. Or that there was someone else involved. You open yourself up to a reinterpretation of events, which can be disorienting.

But therapists agree that this truth-seeking process is essential. When Becky Palmer, a specialist in sexual abuse, counsels sex offenders and victims, she urges the perpetrators to tell the truth in a very specific way, both for their sake and for the victim's. "The first step is getting the offender to acknowledge the facts," she says. "Without that, it's much harder to forgive." She asks the offender to write the victim a letter admitting what happened. "Often this takes months," she says. "They say things like, 'I'm sorry for that thing.' I make them name what it was: having intercourse, fondling, or whatever. I make them name the act."

Palmer points to four typical levels of denial on the part of sexual abusers: denial of facts, denial of awareness, denial of impact, and denial of responsibility. In other words: It didn't happen, I didn't notice it, it didn't matter, and it wasn't my fault.

It seems to me that some victims have their own parallel versions of denial. The first three are the same: It didn't happen, I didn't notice it, it didn't matter. The fourth is a little different: It wasn't his fault. Some victims, especially women, tend to shy away from fully blaming the perpetrator, trying to justify his actions or reduce his responsibility as a way to cushion their own anger.

Yet blame is important. As part of the truth-seeking process, it's important to decide who was responsible for what. You can't forgive someone until you know whom you blame. Often, women unthinkingly and irrationally blame themselves. It's easier, I think, than dealing with the pain of blaming someone who should have loved us, or should have been worthy of our trust, or simply should have respected us more than they did. It's also difficult to blame someone who is dead, or someone who won't admit that they did anything wrong. It's easier—but less productive—to blame ourselves.

Once we do blame someone, it's natural to seek revenge in retaliation for what they have done to us. Even if we don't punish them directly, we might be pleased to learn that they are suffering. There are at least two words for this: the German *schadenfreude*, meaning pleasure derived from the misfortunes of others, and the Hebrew *yetzer*, meaning, according to the Talmud, "that egocentric, selfish, and aggressive part of the personality which delights in seeing one's enemy miserable."

Marny Hall, a therapist and author who lives in Berkeley, California, explains: "Not from a spiritual perspective, but purely from a psychological one, I think people need to express a certain amount of vengeance before they can forgive. I think it's human nature to want to know that the other person has suffered somehow. You have to have some sense that the score has been evened, even if you didn't have a hand in it." In her work with her clients, she might suggest that a child molester, for instance, has probably been alienated from other people or has been tortured by shame. "If a person can see that the other person has not had a golden life, or has had his comeuppance in some way, then it's easier to be grand-spirited later."

A college administrator named Stella felt no desire for vengeance but did find that anger was an inescapable hurdle on her journey toward forgiveness. Stella was born in 1961, placed in an orphanage for six weeks, then adopted. Her adoptive mother "had a lot of anxiety about bonding with me," says Stella. "She seemed driven by an overriding desire to make the relationship the way she imagined a 'natural' one would be. Whenever I was different from her, she saw that as her failure to make me just like her 'real' child."

As a result, mother and daughter "fought all the time." They clashed over how Stella would dress, who her friends would be, what her politics and religion would be. "She did not have the capacity to recognize me for who I was, and to honor me for that. She did many other good things, but I see this as a fundamental deficit."

When Stella gave birth to a child of her own, she started facing her feelings about her two mothers. Her predominant emotion was anger: at her biological mother for abandoning her at birth, and at her adoptive mother for many things, including "disallowing any kind of emotional discussion about the adoption."

"The struggle was to let myself get angry in the first place," she says. "I needed to experience this hurt and anger before I could get anywhere near forgiveness."

Stella located her natural mother when her son was still a baby, but meeting her triggered more anger. During that initial meeting, Stella's natural mother asked Stella whether she was angry at her for giving her away. "I think by asking that question she was trying to apologize," says Stella. "I didn't know in that moment how angry I still was."

Over the course of the next year, Stella attempted to maintain contact, but her mother "didn't seem able or willing to do that." This second rejection generated "recycled" anger and hurt for Stella, who would lament, "She's not calling back! She's not writing back! She's gone again!"

Her pain was typical, notes Stella, who has studied the adoption process. "Adoptees often create an idealized vision of who the birth mother will be, and what the relationship will be like," then get disappointed, she says.

Eventually Stella began to ask herself, "What do I want to do with this anger? Let it suck up my life? Demonize this person?"

She chose to forgive—an ongoing, unfinished process, she says. She now says of her birth mother, "I'm much less angry. Whatever is driving her not to be in touch with me at this time, she's not evil. She has her own reasons, and I must respect her choice. There are still times when I want to say, 'Make a different choice! What's your problem? I'm an interesting person!' but I'm not sure I would really want to push us into a relationship anyway. I probably can't get from her the mothering I'd want."

Her adoptive mother is now in her seventies, "so it's easier to say, 'This is a sick old person, without much more time on the planet,'" says Stella. "She means well and blew it in some ways. I'm in the bloom of life, and I have responsibility for making this be okay now."

Stella can now see, she says, that her adoptive mother is emotionally needy, that she has limitations, that she did the best she could. "I can see her basic humanity. Everybody fucks up."

Tapping into her anger, she says, has taught her that "anger isn't going to kill me." It also showed her that she can get angry with her husband without being abandoned again. "My husband loves me. He made this promise in front of all these people. Now I can get really pissed off, then come back from that and move on to the process of forgiving."

Neither mother has given her the apology she would like, and neither has transformed miraculously into "the mother I needed," Stella says. "But really accepting that that's not going to happen is very important."

It's also important to differentiate between who was responsible then and who is responsible now. Bruce, for instance, is not responsible for how I feel about him now, nor is he responsible for how emotionally healthy I am now. I can reasonably blame him for exploiting me when I was young, but as an adult, I need to take responsibility for my own choices and outlook.

Judith Herman, author of *Trauma and Recovery*, says, "Trauma is resolved only when the survivor develops a new mental 'schema' for understanding what has happened."[1] Dr. O. Carl Simonton calls this "cognitive restructuring." It doesn't always feel like a cognitive process. Some people I interviewed said they discovered forgiveness through prayer, or meditation, or the passage of time. "Suddenly, after praying, I didn't hate him anymore," they would say, or, "I don't know how I forgave him; maybe it's true that time heals." Still, for most of us honest answers about the facts of the case tend to yield a new way of looking at things, a new understanding of who was at fault, who was not at fault, what impact the incident really had, and who is responsible now. Sometimes these answers alter a belief that the world revolves around us. The egocentric view is: *How could they do that to me!?* A more balanced view is: *People do what they do. Sometimes we happen to be there when they vent their rage, express their ignorance, exploit someone for their own gain. This time it happened to be me. If it hadn't been me, they probably would have hurt someone else.*

This perspective can help a person regain dignity and self-worth: *It wasn't really about me after all.* People are who they are. They're not who we want them to be. That's unfortunate, but true.

This brings to mind Bruce's poster: ". . . and if by chance we find each other, it's beautiful." I now think: *And if by chance we hurt each other, it's not really personal.* Bruce molested me because I was available. If I hadn't been there, he would have molested someone else, and indeed, when I moved away he did molest other girls. That doesn't make the injury any less hurtful to me, but it helps me develop a new mental schema for understanding what happened. Once I begin to interpret things less personally, I move closer to forgiveness.

Buddhists take this one step further: Nothing bad happens. Life just is. Consider the person whose leg is broken in a car accident. He might feel angry at the other driver, angry at the maintenance people who failed to clear the roadway, angry at God for making it rain that day, or angry at himself for having driven too fast. Zen guide Cheri Huber, author of *There Is Nothing Wrong with You* and several other books, responds to this hypothetical situation: "Nothing is wrong with this life. He's not supposed to be living some other sort of life in which he didn't break his leg. Our suffering happens when we start to believe that things should be different."

I wish I could, but I can't share that level of universal acceptance—the idea that nothing is wrong. It does seem to me that human beings should behave differently. People should not torture or murder children, for instance. There do seem to be some moral absolutes. Nevertheless, I accept this point: What is, is. What we're given, we're given. How we respond to it is what matters. The Buddhist concept of karma makes sense to me: We are recipients of karmic legacies, forces set in motion before we were born. The best we can do is clean up the karma by being the kindest, gentlest, most forgiving people we can be.

Diana, founder and owner of a successful event management company in Washington, D.C., forgave her family members as she undertook a five-year personal journey she calls "becoming a whole person." A key factor, she says, involved taking a close look at who her parents were, then forgiving them. "I grew up in a family where there was very little nurturing," she recalls. "No one ever told me they loved me until I was eighteen or nineteen years old, and only then because I started making them. My dad was very high-spirited but kept everyone at arm's length. He had very high expectations, and if you didn't meet those expectations, he said you were stupid. My mother is a very distant person. She never touched me. If you got in her space, she would back up. As a result, I had extremely low self-esteem. People didn't know that, because I always looked like this extrovert, very successful, always driving myself to unrealistic levels, but I didn't love myself. I guess as a little girl I thought, 'If your mother can't touch you and never tells you she loves you, you must not be lovable.'"

When she got engaged, Diana asked her father to write her fiancé a letter, welcoming him into the family. She saved the letter. He wrote, "I would like to say I love Diana, but I don't. But I don't feel that about any of my children, but of all my children, she does give me the most plea-sure."

During a low point in her career a few years ago, when Diana was staying in a distant city alone, trying unsuccessfully to make a deal go through, her mother came to visit. Diana said to her mother, "This is the hardest thing I've ever done. I have never failed at anything before. I'm struggling with this new business, and losing money, and I don't have any friends here. I really need someone to touch me. Would you please just give me a hug?" Her mother "couldn't do it," Diana recalls. "Just as she turned to do it, my glasses hit her hearing aid, and that gave her an out."

Emerging from a professional and personal depression, Diana began a long internal process of contemplating who her parents really were, and what had really happened in her family. She now says, "I've forgiven my parents because I figured out where they were coming from. They never meant to hurt me. I just interpreted it that way because I wasn't getting what I needed. My mother's father was workaholic. My mother's mother was the same way she is: no nurturing, no touching, didn't say she loved you. My mother doesn't think like I do, so she has no understanding of who I am, and at eighty-two, if she hasn't figured it out, she isn't going to. I talk to her now the way I always wanted to, but she can't hear me. She says, 'I really don't know what you're talking about.'

"My father's father was alcoholic. My father was an only child, and he didn't learn how to interact. He didn't love himself. He died of a heart attack. I now think that when you die of a heart ailment, you're really dying of a broken heart."

Diana's mother recently knitted her an afghan, "the most beautiful gift you've ever seen, and the only thing she ever gave me that she actu-ally made," says Diana. She wrote her mother a thank-you note, saying, "When you're gone, I'll wrap this around me, and I'll feel your arms." Her mother did not respond to the note. "Because she can't," says Diana. "She doesn't know how. How can you be mad at somebody who doesn't know how?"

Chapter 5

VALIDATION:
LETTING PAIN BE PAIN

*W*hen we started talking again after all those years of silence, Bruce and I reestablished a relationship. It was different from our original relationship: more anger, more tears, less trust. Yet it was also similar to our original relationship: gentle, familiar, heartfelt, and at times confusing. As was true all those years ago, Bruce was a good listener.

This is one of the things potential forgivers need most: To be listened to. To be heard. To communicate our pain and our experience and have someone say, "Yes, I hear you." Ideally, the person who listens is the same person who inflicted the wound. Alternatively, sometimes someone else will do.

By listening, Bruce validated my feelings. I didn't need his confirmation to know that my memory was correct, but his affirming response was far preferable to denial—the response many sexual abuse survivors receive when they confront their perpetrator. I felt lucky that Bruce was willing to deal with my feelings, even the extreme ones. In one letter I wrote:

Dear Bruce,

Hi. It's me again—the writer, writing. To heal, to communicate.

I have a huge amount of anger about what happened, and I'm not sure how to deal with that, so I'm muddling through. But when I express anger it's not in order to make you suffer. I believe you have suffered enough. I'm just not sure *how* to do my own healing process, so I'm making it up as I go, hoping not to cause more pain in the process.

At the same time, if I get too concerned about you and your pain, it makes it harder for me to get in touch with my own feelings, and to express them to you, which seems to be an important part of this process. This is classic female conditioning—taking care of men, even men who have abused us, more than we take care of ourselves. Part of feminism (which you asked about) is learning how to stop putting ourselves second.

One idea of something you and I could possibly do when we meet in person: pray/meditate. We have this in common—a spiritual path—and maybe that could help us.

Buddhists talk about "accepting all that is," and for me that points toward a way that I can integrate and accept all my complicated feelings about the past and present. "What is" for me right now: heartbreak, sorrow, rage, painful memories, shame, fear, grief, vulnerability, relief, openness, excitement, hope. All of these things (and more) mix together and make me ill, literally, with stomachaches. Yes, crying helps.

Many years ago I met a young woman whose parents were both dead. I asked her, "How is that for you?" She said, "I'm okay with it now." I told that story to Margaret, my therapist, and said I'd like to get there regarding my own history of sexual abuse. I'd like to be able to say, "I'm okay with it now." She noted that the word *now* implies that the woman had not always been okay with her parents' death; it had been a *process*.

Mariah

At the end of the letter I thanked Bruce for listening, for answering my questions, for taking responsibility, for not rushing me. I told him that it meant a lot to me that he had said I wouldn't have to go through this alone and now was demonstrating that. I acknowledged that I was giving him mixed messages, explained that I was "muddling through with no road map," and expressed gratitude and optimism about the journey.

Bruce's response, five days later:

Dear Mariah,

I too believe strongly in prayer and would be most happy to share that time with you. I also believe this healing process has begun because of answering prayers.

I am reading a book called *The Final Six Days of Jesus* by Max Lacado. In it he speaks of Judas. It was straight to my heart in the definition of "betrayal." To be betrayed, it cannot come from an enemy. It comes from someone you love and care about—a friend. The betrayal becomes the violation of trust and all that is associated with it. I am so sorry I betrayed you.

We are in "process." It is new to me also. I do feel we are moving and in a good direction. To hear you laugh the other day was refreshing. I listen for that laugh in my mind as I think of us each day. I hope that your "anger, sorrow, rage, shame, fear, and grief" can be cast aside and that each day will bring relief, excitement, hope, and an appreciation of who you have become.

Your mixed messages and mixed feelings are still very welcomed. It would be foolish for both of us to expect that a letter, meeting, or phone call was going to place us in a position of total understanding. I will walk, crawl, or even run with you to get to a time and place where life is filled with peace and understanding.

I again thank you with all my heart for caring enough to try.

You are in my prayers,

Bruce

Several times Bruce asked me to meet him "for lunch." He seemed to believe that if I saw him in person, I would forgive him. He kept assuring me that he had spent the past twenty-five years making up for the wrong he did to me, and that "there are so many people who would say to you, 'He's been the biggest influence for good.'"

At that point, it didn't matter to me how much good he had done for others. But I grew curious to see him. Who was he now compared to who he had been then? Might seeing him somehow help me reach forgiveness?

In retrospect, it was stupid, the way I arranged our first meeting. I was about to deliver a speech to a group of teachers. I arrived at the lecture hall—which happened to be in Bruce's town—and learned that I had almost two hours to wait, alone, before the banquet and speech. I spontaneously called him at work. "I just found out that I'm about five minutes away from you, and I could borrow a car and come say hello," I told him on the phone.

What made me think I could meet with my molester for the first time in twenty-five years, then deliver a speech a few hours later? I've trained myself—largely through sports—to perform under pressure regardless of my emotional state. But I've also learned to deny the impact of his abuse. Underestimating what would happen, I just called him.

He seemed eager. "Yes," he said emphatically. I liked the sound of his yes. It sounded brave, the way a novice sky diver might say yes when asked, "Are you sure you want to leap out of this plane?"

Extremely nervous myself, I could hardly hold my pen as Bruce gave me directions to his office. I got lost on the way there. Then I parked, climbed out of the car, and saw him waiting for me on the far side of the lot. Immediately, I recognized the shape of his head, his gait. He recognized me too. We then endured an interminable walk toward each other—the opposite, in some ways, of the classic romantic reunion in which two people run into each other's arms. But no less emotional. When we finally reached each other, I opened my arms, offering a hug.

I had planned this hug. This is what I had imagined in all my many imaginings of this initial meeting, wherever it might be: that we would hug. It would be a peace offering from me, a comforting show of remorse from him. But it did not go as planned. He collapsed into my arms and dropped his head forlornly onto my shoulder, banging his forehead on my bony clavicle. He was crying. With my nose pressed against his hair, I was astounded by the scent of him: the same combination of chewing gum, cologne, and shampoo that had been so familiar, attractive, and terrifying to me as a teenager. In all those intervening years, I had never thought about his scent, but now, inhaling it, I was transported back to his car, to the locker room, to all the places he molested me. Shame, nausea, fear, and grief overwhelmed me. I tried to talk but could not.

When I released the hug, he gazed at me through his tears, taking both my hands in his and squeezing too tightly, crushing my ring into my index finger. It hurt. When I was finally able to speak, my first words to him were, "You're hurting me." I pulled my hand away, pointing to the place on my finger where my ring had indented the skin. He apologized profusely, muttering something about having hurt me *again* already. Again already, I reassured him that it was okay.

The rest of the visit was equally awkward and, for me, worse. In his office, he offered me a seat, then, to my surprise, sat next to me. I had expected him to sit farther away, behind his desk. My arm was on the armrest, and he placed both of his hands on top of my forearm, touching it firmly, for emphasis and connection. This made me very uncomfortable, but I didn't say anything. I remembered: This is his way, he's a toucher.

In my family, we did not touch much, so I had been fascinated when I began to meet people like Bruce: people who would casually grab your hand to lead you somewhere, touch your shoulder while admiring a blouse, reach out for your arm while laughing. Sitting there with Bruce, I remembered that this was part of his appeal back then. I liked the warmth that came through all that touching. Long before he touched me sexually, he touched me in many ways that felt friendly and kind.

But when you grow up without much touch, you don't learn to say, "Don't touch me." That's what I wanted to say now as Bruce leaned toward me, gripping my arm and saying, with more tears, "Mariah, I'm so sorry I hurt you when you were young, I'm so very sorry."

I wanted to hear that apology. But I felt like a washing machine with an array of emotions sloshing around inside. The sight of him, the scent of him, the feel of his hands on my arm, the awkward hug and painful squeeze of my ring finger, all of these sent me back in time, and the effect was so disorienting I was speechless and also immobilized. I was not able to tell him to take his hands off me, nor was I able to remove my arm from the armrest. As I had done when he touched me inappropriately so many years ago, I simply froze.

So in the space of one brief visit we reenacted the destructive dynamics of our past: He touched me in a way that made me uncomfortable, and I, wanting his apology and not wanting to hurt his feelings, felt catatonic, unable to say no.

Afterward, I drove back to the teachers' meeting, ate dinner with my hosts, gave a forty-five-minute speech, and signed books at a reception. Throughout all of this, I put Bruce out of my mind. I think I managed to be entertaining and inspiring.

But after the speech, I fell apart. That night, after traveling home, I stayed awake crying, soaked in painful childhood memories. The next morning, I started to drive to my usual swimming practice but returned home because I couldn't see the road through my tears. For a week, I was almost incapacitated by emotional distress. During this time, I had to fly to Denver and Iowa City to deliver two more speeches. I cried on all the planes. In my hotel rooms, I suffered from virtually ceaseless sobbing, rage, flashbacks, insomnia, and wrenching stomachaches. I smelled Bruce's scent. I relived the feelings of his hand squeezing my ring finger, his hands on my arm, his hand between my thighs. I recalled the sexual games we had played in the locker room with the lights out. I grieved too, as if my heart were broken. I felt physically ill, on the verge of vomiting.

"What he did to you years ago made you sick," noted Margaret when I finally got back home. "You're finally free to feel those feelings now." Apparently, I was having some sort of post-traumatic stress response triggered by the sight, smell, and feel of Bruce. I was finally experiencing the betrayal by the man I'd thought was my "first lover," finally grieving not only the loss of that love but perhaps also the loss of my own girlhood innocence. I would have felt crazy if I had not met and read about sexual abuse survivors who, as they're finally coming to terms with the abuse, are so debilitated by pain they can barely move. My sobbing was so convulsive I knew why these women had described crawling around the room or huddling in a fetal position in a corner. It was all I could do to pick up the phone from Colorado and Iowa and call my partner, who was immensely helpful and patient. I also called two other friends and, for the first time in my life, two crisis hotlines.

The word *suicide* even came to mind. I say it that way—that the word came to mind—because it seemed like that: It appeared unbidden in my brain. It did not occur to me to take any action toward suicide. But I felt that bad. I thought: *This is why people commit suicide. This is how awful they feel when they do it.*

The day after I visited Bruce in his office, I wrote him this letter:

Dear Bruce,

Today has been very painful, just awful really, filled with grief and tears and rage. Grief for the girl who was sexualized too early, and inappropriately, by the wrong person, in the wrong context. Who was violated. Overwhelming anger at you for doing it. Someday I'd like to tell you how angry I am about every single instance of sexual contact.

I remember one time that first summer (in your car, as usual) when you asked me if I had ever been turned on. I was fourteen. I had no idea what you were talking about. Really, I was a total innocent. I sensed it had something to do with sex, and I wanted to impress you, so I said yes. It might be the only time I've ever lied to you. Your question in itself was a violation of my privacy.

Last night I couldn't sleep I was so angry about that one simple question—and that was before I even got to my anger about the actual sexual contact. I wish I had said, "It's none of your damn business." Or, "What the hell are you talking about?" Or, "What right do you have to ask me that?" Instead I tried to please you and impress you because I loved you and wanted you to love me.

I'm surprised by the depth of my feelings today, by the pain of it. "Moving toward a possible reconciliation or peace" sounds so much more pleasant than what I'm going through. Forgiveness sounds lovely. I hadn't anticipated that I'd have to move through this pain, not around it.

If there's one primary need I have identified so far, it's to have you listen to me. And you have convinced me that you are listening.

Mariah

Shortly after my return from the trip to Denver and Iowa, I received this reply from Bruce:

Dear Mariah,

After reading about your pain, my overwhelming sense of sorrow and remorse has taken on an even greater depth. To continue to cause you pain, anger, and grief is difficult to manage for a person who has a conscience and cares.

Mariah, please don't give up on "moving toward a possible reconciliation or peace" and forgiveness. I will continue to listen and feel the pain you have. My selfish hope is that you will be able to recognize this and know that I have felt your pain for a long, long time.

I sense that you are a caring, loving person who would like to move on from the experiences of the past. I will do everything I can to help you with this.

Just as the sun rises each morning with the promise of a new day, each letter, each call, each contact holds the promise of a new relationship.

Take good care of yourself, and thanks for taking the time to write. I am thankful,

Bruce

He told me, in essence, "I feel your pain." I'm not sure someone can actually feel someone else's pain, but the fact that Bruce was listening helped enormously. I believed that he cared, and I found this attentiveness very healing.

This is where "liberation begins," the theologian Matthew Fox has said: "at the point where pain is acknowledged and allowed to be pain."[1] Bruce allowed my pain to be pain.

I was fortunate in that way. Though it took him more than twenty years, eventually he made himself available to help me resolve my old wounds. I was also fortunate to have access to a therapist who provided a more reliable and uncomplicated validation of my pain. I think Margaret understood just how much Bruce had hurt me even before I did. When she referred to that ("he really hurt you deeply") I would recoil at first, since I had never really let myself believe that and had always defended against the pain by convincing myself it had not been a big deal. But she witnessed my breakdown and saw me tearful and nauseated for several weeks afterward, and she later saw how hard it was for me to face him in our special two-hour therapy session. I stayed in therapy for more than two years, and though I talked about other things, I'd estimate that 90 percent of the work was related to Bruce: what happened then and the effect it was having on me. I felt like she understood. I felt seen. I felt heard. And I believed she saw my strength as well as my pain. All of this too was tremendously validating.

We want the wrongdoer to understand exactly what they did wrong and how it hurt us. If we can't obtain this understanding from them, we may remain stuck. A computer artist name Steve, for instance, talked to me about his craving for validation from two sources: a boss who had been verbally abusive, and a girlfriend who had declared that they were "soul mates," then abruptly announced she was marrying someone else.

"I would have fantasies of hurtful things happening to them," he admits. "Or when very minor bad things happened to them, I felt some gratification. I grew to realize these spontaneous feelings were not really what I wanted for these people. I wanted them to feel and understand my pain—the pain I suffered at their hands. I wanted validation, empathy, and most of all, understanding. That was my ultimate goal.

"In fact, that's my only goal. I feel no animosity toward these people. I really wish no bad things for them. I just want a good thing for me: recognition and understanding. But since they can't or won't be part of that, my emotions hit a brick wall and get bent into hostility, into thinking I want to hurt them. Since I have not had any resolution to my feelings, I still feel moments of deep insult and anger."

While writing this book, I became one vehicle through which people had their pain validated. This was not my intent, but I noticed a pattern: People were eager to be interviewed. More so than any group of people I've interviewed on other subjects, people returned my phone calls, even calling me repeatedly if I did not contact them again right away. For the most part, these people were in the "have not forgiven" group, as opposed to the "have forgiven" group. Later I realized that the two groups overlapped, with many people in the middle. But mostly it was the nonforgiving ones who kept calling and who would willingly reschedule when the need arose, even during one winter storm season when power outages, burst water pipes, and other problems interrupted our plans.

Stella, the adopted child who is in the process of forgiving both of her mothers, explained her interest in our interview: "Talking is how I understand things. The more I tell this story, the more proficient I become at understanding it, thinking it through clearly, seeing the emotional pieces that might still be unresolved. It's gratifying that I can now tell it as well as I can." For her, the very act of talking about forgiveness seemed to make her a more forgiving person. "Talking about forgiveness is like practicing it, like doing it," she said.

Archbishop Desmond Tutu noticed a similar dynamic with the Truth and Reconciliation Commission: "Very many of those who came forward found the telling, just the telling itself, very cathartic, very healing," he said.

Steve also seemed eager to share his story. Neither his boss nor his ex-girlfriend had apologized to him, and he had not forgiven them, though he said he had made some progress toward that goal. As we were concluding our third interview, I said to him, "I wonder what your motivation was to participate in these conversations. You called me several times. It seems maybe you were looking for something from this process."

After some thought, he said, "Validation. It's useful to have you validate my anger and acknowledge my side of the story, even though you weren't involved. It seems cathartic. Especially since I can't get that from my boss or my ex-girlfriend, there's a satisfaction in having someone hear me and believe me."

"Do you think that might help you move toward forgiveness?" I asked.

"Yes," he said.

Stella and Steve helped me clarify why people were eagerly calling me: It's useful to have someone—almost any kind person—offer a sympathetic ear: to say, "Yes, it happened; it was awful or unjust or hurtful; I see why you're upset." If the perpetrator would say, sympathetically, "I'm so sorry I did that, and I can understand why you feel that way, and you must be really hurting right now," that's ideal, but when, more typically, the perpetrator won't or can't fulfill this need, it's useful to have someone else do it.

Often, therapy is the first place where people feel heard and validated. When therapy works, I think this is a major reason why. Therapists act as witnesses to our pain, sometimes counteracting other people in our lives, or other voices in our heads, telling us that it didn't matter, or it wasn't bad, or we shouldn't care. From a therapist we hear, "I see that you're hurting, and I see why, and it matters."

Therapy is also where some of us first feel forgiven. Therapists try not to be judgmental or blaming; in general, they try to offer what Carl Rogers called "unconditional positive regard." Some patients experience this as a healing, pure sort of love. In good therapeutic relationships, clients can begin to forgive themselves when they confess wrongdoing (short of criminal activity) and feel forgiven by the therapist.

Thus, many therapists probably routinely witness something that came as a surprise to me as an interviewer. The more I listened, the more people changed their stories, moving along a continuum from not-forgiving toward forgiving. Several times people began interviews by telling me they had *not* forgiven someone, then, after talking about it for forty-five minutes or so, ended up saying that they *had* forgiven that person. I was not coaching them. I was not acting like a therapist—except to listen. At first I thought they were merely confused or ambivalent, expressing a complex forgiving/not forgiving perspective all at once. But then, studying transcripts, I began to see a pattern: They might have started out confused or uncertain, but as we talked they moved closer to forgiveness, sometimes just in the space of one conversation.

Joyce, for instance, originally told me that she had not forgiven her ex-lover, Alison, for having an affair and lying to her about it. "Do I forgive this woman? Hell, no. I'm still mad when I think about it," she said at the outset. Over the course of our interview, as she explained in sordid detail all the hurts and betrayals, she asked rhetorically, "How could I forgive all that?" Yet toward the end of our talk, she started saying more compassionate things, like, "I truly believe she had no clue of the way she was treating me. I don't think she was deliberately hurting me." Finally, Joyce talked about her pain in the past tense, saying, "It's almost as if the hurt isn't there anymore," and even, "I would have to say I have forgiven her. I'm no longer trapped by the emotions. I'm ready to move on."

Could I have been influencing Joyce, and others, with my questions or comments? Could they have sensed my attitude about forgiveness and deliberately or subconsciously been trying to please me? Could my questions have helped them think about things in new ways, which immediately opened them to a more forgiving perspective? Or was the listening itself the most powerful force?

Surely my interviewees had a general sense that I was "for" forgiveness, and some might have wanted to please me. My questions might have helped some of them think about things, or feel things, in a different way. To ask about compassion or sympathy for the offender, which I often did, is to plant a seed. One woman even told me later, "Your challenging questions have been a great gift to me. You are helping me unscramble a lot of this, and make sense of it, and most of all evolve into a healthier place." To the degree that I was helping people evolve to a healthier place merely by asking a few questions, that's good news about how easily forgiveness can happen once you start to think about it and discuss it.

Sometimes all I did was listen. I heard a joke once about a patient who goes to see a psychiatrist once a week for ten years. During each visit, the patient lies on the couch and talks for an hour, then leaves. The psychiatrist never says a word. At the end of the ten years, the patient stands up and says, "Thanks, Doctor! I feel so much better!" The joke is funny because of the truth in it: Being listened to is incredibly powerful and healing.

Sometimes I was like the psychiatrist who says nothing, not because of my own professional commitment to silence, but because for many of these people the need to tell their story was so great that I couldn't have asked questions if I tried. They just talked, on and on and on. Then sometimes, at the end of our session, they'd say, in effect, "I feel so much better!"

About six months after my initial series of conversations with Steve, the computer artist, I called him back to check in. I reminded him that we had discussed the potentially healing effects of our interviews, and now I was wondering: Did our conversations indeed lead to any enduring sense of resolution? Did he feel any lighter, or less angry? And to what degree would he now say he'd forgiven his boss and ex-girlfriend?

"Talking about it definitely helped," Steve said, "especially because I sensed the listener was empathetic and not judgmental. Yes, I feel less angry. Much less. It will always be part of my history. Now it's just old furniture up in the attic, instead of in my living room.

"I wish I could say I have forgiven them. That would be the nice and kind thing to do. But I have trouble with the concept of forgiving someone for something they are in denial about, and have no cognizance of, and can't conceive of apologizing for.

"But I feel very, very content. I feel no obligation to forgive them. Their offenses, their callousness, their crimes, are their issues. My issue is how I separate from these people. My issue is how I deal with my feelings. My issue is how I recognize the limits of my power. I can't make them feel or behave the way I want them to feel or behave."

At that point, unprompted by me, Steve began talking about the next key to forgiveness and freedom: compassion. "It must be difficult, living their lives," he said. "I don't know how well I would cope if I had their burdens, if I had to carry the weight they have. Man, this sounds creepy, but when I am past any anger I have for them, I actually feel bad for them. And the fact that I can empathize with my villain—I believe there is strength and grace in that. Somehow I feel my humanity confirmed and actually strengthened. I think this is part of why I feel content, and why I have a sense of resolution."

Steve didn't achieve all this insight and peace simply from talking to me. He has been attending forgiveness workshops, seeing a psychologist, and spending a lot of time thinking about this. But I now believe that validation is an essential and overlooked key to forgiveness and freedom. Traumatic experiences and emotions seem to be most effectively processed when shared with other human beings. Later, after receiving validation for your own pain, you can begin to "empathize with the villain," contemplating the pain of the person who inflicted the injury.

Chapter 6

COMPASSION: SEEKING THE HUMANITY IN OTHERS

My friend Kimberly Carter says, "Behind every jerk there's a sad story."

Steve's boss, for instance, is just such a jerk. Steve, the computer artist, worked for this "irrationally critical" man for three years. "His anger would be triggered by the slightest thing," Steve recalls. "He would call me into his office for private, closed-door 'disciplinary' meetings, during which he always lost control of his anger." Shaking and perspiring, with his voice raised, the boss "would begin with vague innuendo, then level wild accusations at me. I would stand up for myself, but he never acknowledged my comments. It was frightening, a threat to my sense of survival. I was in a constant state of fear and stress." As a result, Steve developed insomnia, facial tics, a faulty memory, and a stutter.

The bizarre part—and the part that revealed the sad story behind the jerk—was that toward the end of these meetings the boss would talk about how his father had treated him when he was young. "He described a pattern of abuse that was identical to how he treated me. He would even use the same language. He'd say, 'My father picked on me,' then he'd say, 'I'm not picking on you.'

"He never seemed to make the connection, but it was clear," says Steve. "My friends would say, 'Tell him not to burden you with his personal problems,' but I liked listening. It explained a lot. I know for a fact that he was treated worse than he treated me. Although this doesn't excuse his behavior, it was a little bit easier for me once I understood him."

Finally Steve quit his job and "moved to a profession where I was not as competent or skilled and don't have such natural gifts. I also took a pay cut."

He started seeing a psychologist, who told him that "no one is hostile unless they have been treated badly themselves." That insight helped Steve develop some compassion for his boss. "Even though I hated this person more than anyone I've ever had to deal with, if I had the opportunity to save his life, I would do it," he says. "At least that's something."

Kipland Kinkel, the fifteen-year-old Oregonian who in May 1998 was charged with killing his parents and two classmates and injuring twenty-two others, explained in a note found in his locker: "Killers start sad."

Killers start sad, abusive bosses were abused themselves, our enemies' hearts are full of sorrow. People with happy home lives and high self-esteem do not hurt others intentionally. Cruelty does not emerge from joy and contentment. Hence, a person who wounds someone else, whether deliberately or not, is a candidate for compassion. Even trivial offenders qualify. The colleague who teases you about your clothes or your nose probably feels insecure about her own clothes or nose, or is jealous of your salary, or never felt loved by her mom. Behind every jerk there's a sad story.

Whatever the circumstances, there is a sad story. There are reasons why people rear-end your car or steal your silverware or bully your son or neglect to send you a wedding invitation. No one is hostile unless they have been treated badly themselves. Everyone deserves compassion.

The word *compassion* comes from the Latin "to suffer with." First a victim "suffers with" himself—with his physical or emotional wounds, with the parts that were injured. Then he notices that both he and his offender are hurting, and he starts to "suffer with" the offender. As he becomes aware of the pain of the person who hurt him, the doors of his heart begin to open.

During my forgiveness process with Bruce, I got confused sometimes, thinking about his needs and my needs. Friends warned me to watch out for myself. "Don't worry about him," they said. But what sort of person would I be if I didn't worry or care about him—or anyone? Can't I do both? I wondered. Can't I be compassionate for Bruce and for myself at the same time?

Cheri Huber says compassion is "the beginning and ending point of spiritual practice." Instead of going to confession, she urges, "go to compassion."

It's an appealing destination. Regarding Bruce, I wanted to get there because caring feels better than seething and makes me feel better about myself. This desire to care, and even to assist, is not unusual among victims of various crimes, says professional mediator Mark Umbreit. He wrote his doctoral dissertation on the meaning of fairness among victims of juvenile burglary. "I was surprised by how much compassion was shown by victims," he says. "Their primary concern was to help the kids. There's way more forgiveness out there than we realize."

Were the victims compassionate because the perpetrators were young? Perhaps. It's often easier to see vulnerability and neediness in a child than in an adult. People also use age as a justification for vengefulness: "He's old enough to have known better!" But in fact, people don't automatically "know better" when they become legal adults. Those who want to feel compassionate for an adult might try imagining that the adult is still a child, or still acting from an immature attitude, or acting in some misguided way that was learned in childhood.

The South African principle of *ubuntu* ("seeking the humanity in others") guided the unprecedented and controversial hearings conducted by Archbishop Desmond Tutu and his Truth and Reconciliation Commission throughout 1997 and 1998. Whether in a political or personal context, this is how people move beyond grudges, hatred, and violence and toward truth and reconciliation: through seeking the humanity in others. It's good for a country's healing process, and it's good for an individual's healing process. By acting compassionate—even for someone related to the offender, or even for an offender who is uncooperative and unrepentant—you become a more compassionate person. By remembering that your enemy is human, you become more human yourself.

"I try to live how God wants me to live."

Bruce said that, and other things like that. His words impressed me because they sounded sincere. His religious convictions made me feel closer to him, and more trusting. We were speaking the same essential language of intentional goodness. When I thought about the situation in terms of justice and injustice, I felt angry. When I thought about it from a psychological perspective, I felt sad. But when I drew on my spiritual practice, my path became clear: Of course I should forgive.

When I told my friend Nancy Croteau about my conversations with Bruce, she said, "That sounds like very important work. Child molesters are people too. We've done lots for victims, and lots for sex offenders, but not much in terms of creating dialogue and understanding between the two. If we're going to get beyond this problem, people are going to have to try to understand each other."

Yet Bruce told me many things I found difficult to hear. When I was a teenager, he had said that he didn't think of me as a teenager, that I was "mature enough to handle it," that it was "okay to love more than one person at the same time," and that sex was a "gift" to me. That some of these justifications were still valid to him two decades later infuriated me. Though I gradually broke through some of his defenses, Bruce also annoyed me by lapsing into self-pity, complaining about how difficult his life was now. He acted victimized by the fact that I had, in effect, forced him to "come out" as a child molester to his family, boss, and colleagues, as if the pain he experienced in those relationships were somehow my fault. Theoretically, I wanted to understand him, but in practice some of his attitudes just made me angrier.

Along this bumpy route, I noticed something that fascinated me: You can't feel critical and compassionate at the same time. You might be angry, then have a glimpse of compassion, then go back to being angry. But in that one moment when your heart opens, you can't be angry too.

Bernhard Schlink explains this in his novel *The Reader*. As the protagonist struggles to sort out his feelings for a former Nazi guard whom he had once loved, he says, "I wanted simultaneously to understand Hanna's crime and to condemn it. But it was too terrible for that. When I tried to understand it, I had the feeling I was failing to condemn it as it must be condemned. When I condemned it as it must be condemned, there was no room for understanding. . . . I wanted to pose myself both tasks—understanding and condemnation. But it was impossible to do both."[1]

Understanding a crime—or a misdemeanor, or a simple thoughtless remark—does not mean that we can't disapprove of the offending behavior, or hold the person responsible, or swear never to do it ourselves. It does, however, soften the condemnation. Once we seek and find someone's humanity, it's impossible to judge them quite so harshly.

Even when the wounds are just small cuts, and even when the offenders are our well-intentioned friends, family members, or colleagues, seeking the humanity in others can be difficult. It can be difficult to let go of our own hurt long enough to consider the other person and what they might be going through. It can be difficult to listen to someone else's experience when their perspective only insults and enrages us further. Often, we're too angry or fearful to reach out and seek someone else's humanity. It's far easier to stay in the victim role, feeling righteous and indignant.

It can also be confusing to sort out: *Can I condemn the behavior but empathize with the person? Can I open my heart but remain wary of being hurt again? Can I forgive but not reconcile?*

So where to start? With compassion for yourself. With your own pain, and with tenderness for that pain, rather than the judgments that so many of us make about our pain: *I shouldn't be angry in the first place; I shouldn't be angry anymore; I shouldn't have felt so hurt; it wasn't really so bad.* "Suffer with" yourself, as if holding your own hand, or hugging yourself, letting your own pain be pain. This self-caring gives you practice in the act of compassion and offers the possibility of overflow compassion, extra feelings of empathy that can later spill out toward another person.

When the exact nature of your experience has been expressed and validated, when your emotions have been honored and soothed and cared for, then eventually the time comes to gently shift the focus away from yourself and ask some questions about the other person. This seems crucial to forgiveness: to get beyond your own concerns, even for a moment, and imagine how life might be for another person, to acknowledge that that person has wounds too, albeit often invisible.

So: Who hurt you? How was that person feeling at the time? What was their life experience that led them to that point? How did they feel about themselves afterward? These are not questions you can approach when consumed by sadness, grief, or rage. But they're powerful questions, and essential steps, I believe, along the path to seeking and finding the humanity in others.

The other person has probably had a rough life, or at least a rough day. As I wrote in the "Conversation" poem, a rapist is not a "happy man." Even the minor offender—the person sitting next to you and your date in the restaurant who snorts every four seconds, for instance—is probably suffering from something, if only allergies.

"If we could read the secret history of our enemies, we should find in each person's life sorrow and suffering enough to disarm all hostility," wrote Henry Wadsworth Longfellow.

A law enforcement officer named Jim Melo offered me an extreme and almost miraculous example of this. Melo's four-year-old daughter Samantha, a "very happy child, a bubble of joy," was killed when she and her car seat were thrown through the windshield during a head-on collision in rural Florida. Samantha's mother, Kathleen, was driving that car. She survived. Jim and Kathleen were separated at the time, and both were dating other people. Their divorce was set to be finalized in just five days. Police said Kathleen had had at least eight drinks before she and her daughter got in the car. The car seat was not strapped in. The driver of the other car was permanently injured. Jim had been expecting to gain custody of Samantha immediately after the divorce.

Forgiveness "started the night of the accident," says Melo, and it started with rage. When he arrived at the hospital where his daughter's body lay, he warned the doctors: "You'd better hope that my gun is not in my car, because I'll kill Kathleen."

Then he was asked to identify Samantha's body. It was wrapped almost completely in white bandages stained with blood. There was a tube in her mouth. Her head was cut in half. He stood silently with his father, his fiancé, his brother, and a doctor. No one spoke. Finally someone asked gently, "Jim, is that Samantha?"

"How the fuck can I tell?" he shouted—a comment for which he now tries to forgive himself. His father nodded to the doctor, and the group left.

A reverend offered to pray with Jim in the hospital waiting room. "Why don't you go in and pray with Samantha?" Jim retorted. "When you and Samantha walk out that door, then you and God will have done something." Jim tries to forgive himself for that remark too.

But something had happened during that encounter with Samantha's mangled body. As he stood looking at what remained of his daughter, his rage at his wife intensified. Then he heard Samantha speaking to him. "The words were so vivid and clear, I almost said, 'What?'" recalls Melo.

Samantha's words: "Daddy, please don't hurt my mommy."

Soon afterward, Melo made plans to drive to another hospital, where Kathleen lay recovering from her injuries. He felt it was his duty to inform her that Sam had not survived. "I didn't want a state trooper to do that," he recalls, "but people were worried that I was going to kill her." By now, however, Melo was calmer, and committed to fulfilling his daughter's request. "I donated Sam's organs and put my sorrow behind me. I have a military background. You see tragedy, you learn to pick up the pieces and move forward."

He drove to the hospital, held his wife's hand, "and spoke to her in a gentle tone, explaining what had happened."

Later, at a meeting to plan Sam's memorial service, some of Melo's family members expressed their own rage, hoping Jim's wife would be sentenced to life in prison. Then Jim spoke up: "I've gotten in a car when I was inebriated. I could have had an accident. Everybody here has driven drunk. It just didn't happen to us." His compassion shocked his family members into silence.

Kathleen was sentenced to three years in prison, served eighteen months, then returned to the same small Florida community where the accident had happened. She ignored an interview request from me. Her attorney, Peter Bell, told the *Sun Herald* that his client "has taken the position that the whole thing is not as her ex-husband is suggesting."

Jim is now happily remarried and has been "blessed" with another daughter. He and Samantha's mother have no deliberate contact. If they see each other in the grocery store, Melo reports, "I don't say anything. My mom always said if you have nothing nice to say, keep your mouth shut."

The pain of losing Samantha "never goes away," he says. "You learn to live with the pain."

Melo says he "cannot" fully forgive the woman who is now his ex-wife. Kathleen has never apologized, he says, nor has she given him some videotapes of Samantha that he longs to have. He finds these things, along with the accident itself, unforgivable. Nevertheless, he has tried to put himself in her shoes. "No one can be that cold, that closed, that silent. If I could be a little man and run around in her brain, then I might forgive her, because then I could understand what her feelings were."

He gives her the benefit of the doubt. "No one will ever convince me she planned to kill my child. She made the mistake of her life, and she has to live with it. I would not want to switch places in a million years."

This is precisely why compassion is so difficult. It involves switching places, at least in our minds, with people who have done things we find deplorable. Compassion "involves tapping into the ghastly potential within ourselves to be cruel and predatory," says psychologist Ann Rasmussen. "In order to really develop compassion, you have to put yourself inside the other person, to identify with her or him, then come back into yourself, in a back-and-forth manner. Part of what makes forgiving others so painful is that it often entails confronting the cruel potential in ourselves in the process."

The key is to find the common denominator with the person you're trying to forgive. If you have been betrayed, then examine the ways you have betrayed others. If you have been lied to, remember your own lies.

In the popular Spike Lee movie *He Got Game,* the father, Jake (played by Denzel Washington), is a likable character, shown shooting hoops in the prison yard, then being welcomed home by his young daughter when he is temporarily released from prison. During flashbacks, we see Jake teaching his son to play basketball—and to control his anger when taunted. By the time we see Jake accidentally kill his wife, he has become a sympathetic character, so we focus on the "accidental" part, not the "kill" part. He didn't mean to do it. She hit her head on a hard kitchen counter. Yes, he had been physically assaulting his young son, and when she tried to stop him he had assaulted her and thrown her down in the kitchen. But . . . he didn't mean to kill her. He assaulted her only that one time, as far as we know. We don't see her parents or siblings mourning or raging. We see only Jake's bleak prison existence, and the flashbacks of his young adulthood, and his sweet relationship with his daughter, and we feel sorry for him. Observing this attractive man, many viewers forgive Jake for this crime and want his son, now a high school senior, to forgive him too—as he eventually does.

This is when forgiveness is easiest: When the wrongdoer is likable. When it was a mistake. When he does not seem evil or repeatedly cruel. When we can see him in context, including his good qualities. And of course, when his wrongdoing involved neither us personally nor people we love.

Usually forgiveness takes more work. The author Gerald Jampolsky offers a humanity-seeking exercise called "Person-to-Person" in which people look into each other's eyes, searching for indications of peace, gentleness, and love. "In other words, we seek their innocence, not their guilt. We look at them with our heart, not our preconceived notions."[2]

Katrina Henderson was looking with her heart when she went to visit Larry Mahoney in prison. Mahoney is the bus driver responsible for the worst drunk driving wreck in the nation's history. He served more than nine years in prison for killing twenty-seven people when his pickup crashed into a school bus near Carrollton, Kentucky, in 1988. Sixty-seven people were returning from a church outing to a Cincinnati amusement park when Mahoney's pickup struck their bus. The collision ruptured the bus's fuel tank, and the victims died from the ensuing fire.

Henderson, one of the survivors, is now a young woman and already a divorced mother of two. She was twelve at the time of the crash. She escaped without physical injury but suffered from recurring nightmares about being trapped in confined spaces. "I've also had nightmares about drowning," she says. "It's all about not being able to breathe. Now in the dreams it's not me that's trapped. It's my kids."

She testified at Mahoney's trial, then wondered about him for years afterward. Finally, in 1995, she wrote him a letter requesting a meeting.

She and a crash survivor who had been badly burned drove to the prison together. "We viewed him as a monster," said Henderson. "I wanted to get past that."

The meeting lasted ninety minutes. Mahoney seemed remorseful. Henderson invited him to appear with her at drunk driving forums when he got out of prison. He agreed. "The visit helped me realize that he is a person," she said. "I don't hate him."[3]

By telling Mahoney of her pain, Henderson's received validation of her own experience. By listening to his remorse, she gave him an opportunity to establish a human connection with one of his victims. By inviting him to speak in public with her, she gave him permission to change—by helping to prevent future accidents. Henderson sought his humanity and found it, learning that he was a person, not a monster.

In the process of seeking that humanity, she also contributed to it. When she visited him and talked with him, she implicitly appealed to his higher self: not the out-of-control drunk, but the considerate person who might (and indeed did) care enough to listen, to express remorse, and to offer to do what he could to help.

Must we reach an understanding of what motivated the other person? Does their offensive behavior have to make sense somehow before we can become compassionate? No. Some people can forgive without attaining any particular intellectual understanding of the other person's motivation. Some people experience forgiveness as an automatic process, or a religious process, or something that simply happens over time.

I never did figure out why Bruce did what he did, though I tried. At first I wondered: Was he an evil child molester? Or a nice guy who made a big mistake? Which was it? If he was basically evil, why had I seen him as caring and kind? Could my teenage perceptions have been that wrong? But if he was a basically good man who made some big mistakes, why hadn't he contacted me during all those silent years? Why hadn't he ever called to say, "I'm sorry, how are you, is there anything I can do to help?" I asked him why he had never contacted me. "Maybe I was afraid," he said.

Maybe he was. But when I asked more questions about why he had molested me, his answers didn't satisfy me. He said he had been a young adult with young children, under a lot of pressure at work and at home. He said he knew our relationship was morally wrong but justified it to himself because I wasn't saying no. He said he liked me and never meant to hurt me. His explanations didn't add up. They sounded like excuses and denial. My mistrust was compounded when his actions and his comments were contradictory: He would seem extremely kind and generous one moment, defensive and self-pitying the next.

Searching for understanding, I told my friend Kimberly Carter, "I can't figure out if he's basically a good guy or basically a bad guy. If he's sincerely sorry and has suffered from guilt all these years, why didn't he ever contact me until after I confronted him?"

She listened carefully. "Oh, that's just human," she said.

Oh, yeah. Apologizing only after someone confronts us: That's just human. We all do it. We do something wrong, then hope no one notices, or hope they forget, or try to forget ourselves. Few of us follow along behind ourselves, cleaning up as we go.

Suddenly, I saw that all of Bruce's behavior was "just human." Defensiveness, rationalizations, self-pity, feeling victimized even when at fault—I've done all those things too, and I will surely do them again.

And what about the sexual exploitation itself? Experts say there are two kinds of child molesters: preferential pedophiles, who are attracted primarily to children, and situational molesters, who have normal adult relationships but also sometimes lack the willpower or moral commitment to set healthy limits in their relationships with young people. I think Bruce was in the second category.

So why did he molest me? Maybe he wanted sex, or a distraction from his work-related or family-related worries, or a feeling of masculine power or virility. Maybe he actually loved me, or liked me a lot, and deluded himself into thinking that there would be no real harm done if our mutual affection were expressed sexually. Maybe, at twenty-five, twenty-six, and twenty-seven, he lacked the maturity to make a good decision about what sort of relationship we should have. Maybe he can't explain it because he doesn't understand it himself.

In any case, I was available. He took advantage of me. That's just human too. Deplorable, yes, but human. This behavior is more characteristic of men—to "take" sex whenever they can get it, including from children—but I've made many poor sexual decisions myself. I can't fully explain why any of us do any of these things, but Kimberly was right. She jarred me into cutting Bruce a little slack, and also somehow cutting myself a little slack in my struggle to understand him. He was both good and bad. He was my friend and he was my exploiter. He tried to take care of me and he tried to take care of himself, albeit in a distorted, unsuccessful way. And in our adult contact, he was again trying to take care of me and also trying to take care of himself.

In my attempt to understand Bruce, I remembered that I was dealing with a human being, not a monster. I switched the focus, for a while, from me to him. I remembered that there are many different human beings on the planet, many life experiences, many points of view.

Bruce was right about this: Having personal contact with him did help me heal. Despite the awkward hug, despite the too-hard squeezing of my hands, despite the unwanted arm-touching in his office and my emotional breakdown afterward, I did see and remember the good parts of him. He wasn't perfect; he still did things that hurt and confused and angered me. But his caring came through. I saw his humanity. I saw his remorse. I began to realize that he had hurt me because of his own limitations as a human being—limitations that were still manifesting themselves in his insensitive forms of touch, in his defensiveness, in his all-too-human attempts to blame his behavior on somebody else.

What if the other person is not available to answer your questions? What if you can't imagine what made them do what they did, and they won't or can't talk to you about it? One option is to interview people who have done similar things and ask them. Or you might talk to the person's friends or family about the person's behavior.

I also think you can invent answers. You can imagine what needs your offender was trying to fulfill when offending you. You can speculate about what that person's inner life was like, what sort of pain or confusion or ignorance might have colored their choices. If you're really courageous, you can try to see in their behavior something with which you can identify, then ask yourself the same questions: What's going on in my life when I act like that? Or what would have to be going on in my life for me to act like that?

Imagine the man in the grocery store who slices into your shin, hard, with his cart. Then, while you're hopping on one foot in agony, he disappears around the corner without saying a word. A hit-and-run shopper. Take care of that shin for a moment—have compassion for yourself—then open your mind and heart and wonder: What is that man's life like? What is he angry about? Did his wife leave him that morning, taking both kids and half the furniture? Are his hemorrhoids killing him? Can he see clearly? Maybe he's losing his vision and terrified about it. Maybe he bumped into someone once before, because of the failing eyesight, and apologized, but the victim caused a scene and humiliated him, so now he's running. Maybe he's scared of you because you're young or tall or muscular or frowning. Maybe he's desperate to find a bathroom because he's having an attack of diarrhea. Maybe you didn't realize it, but you came around that corner pretty fast yourself. Many explanations are possible. All begin to open the heart. All shift the focus from how awful the perpetrator is to how the perpetrator is probably also suffering in his own dysfunctional and invisible way. You'll never get a chance to talk to him about it; by the time you find a Band-Aid, he's left the store. But you can imagine, and in that imagining lie the seeds of forgiveness. This process works with dead people too, or family members who refuse to talk to you about the past. It works because to wonder, in an openhearted way, about another person's life inevitably leads to compassion, which is one key to forgiveness and freedom.

What if the other person isn't suffering? What about the boys in Littleton, Colorado, who laughed as they killed a teacher and students? Witnesses said they seemed to enjoy taunting and slaughtering their peers. Some people do seem callously and zealously to gratify their own needs at the expense of others. If they're discharging sexual or aggressive tension, they may feel a sense of relief. Or power. Or manliness. They may simply be insane.

So maybe it's wrong to assume that people hurt others only because of their own unresolved pain. Not everyone suffers from a guilty conscience. Some people have defense mechanisms that are powerful enough to prevent them from believing they did anything wrong.

But in those cases, what is it like to be that ignorant, that defended, that remote from the impact of your actions on other people? If a person blocks out guilt, doesn't he also block out love? Imagine a person who is insensitive, unable to feel remorse, a person who literally doesn't care about others. How good can insensitivity feel? Isn't that person also a candidate for compassion?

Robert Willie, the man who abducted and raped Debbie Morris and killed at least one other woman, had been arrested thirty times before the age of twenty-one. When Morris asked Sister Helen Prejean whether Willie had shown any remorse before he died, Prejean shook her head sadly and said, "No. And you know, Debbie, I'm not sure he was capable of that."[4]

What sort of person is arrested thirty times before the age of twenty-one? A bad person, unworthy of compassion? Or a seriously disturbed, misguided child? What sort of person is unable to express remorse, even at death's door? A severely limited person, surely. Isn't that severely limited person deserving of compassion?

When Morris grew up, she chose to work with mentally and emotionally disturbed schoolchildren. Getting to know these children, and seeing that they lacked both self-restraint and conscience, she began to realize she was surrounded by some potential Robert Willies. "Unless something happened to turn them around, I believed a lot of these kids were headed for the same sort of serious trouble a few years down the road," she said.[5]

During Willie's trial, she says,

I was conflicted. And the farther Robert Willie's case went, the more conflict I felt. I knew better than almost anyone what kind of evil he had done, but I'd also seen enough of him that I couldn't view him as some theoretical, faceless monster. He was a human being. That meant he had been created in the image of God, so there had to be a part of him that wasn't all bad. He had once been someone's little boy. It was just that somewhere something had gone wrong.[6]

The person Morris had trouble forgiving was Willie's mother, who, according to Morris, gave false testimony at his trial. Yet when Morris had a child of her own, she realized that her own fierce protectiveness might lead her to behave the same way.

* * *

Most of us can't immediately open our hearts to the person who hurt us. But we might be able to care about his mother or wife or kids. Sometimes people refer to this fact sarcastically, saying about someone they deplore: "I don't feel sorry for him, but I do feel sorry for his wife." It's meant to be funny—poor wife, having to live with that jerk—but it seems to me that we often want to extend sympathy to *someone,* even when we can't do it for the person who hurt us.

Families of murder victims sometimes argue against the death penalty on this basis: They don't want the families of the convicted felons to face as much agony as they themselves have known firsthand. Their compassion for other family members—even if not for the perpetrator himself—motivates them to plead for mercy for those who killed their loved ones.

I've noticed a related dynamic I'll call surrogate forgiveness: extending compassion toward, and in a sense forgiving, someone close to the person who hurt you, or someone who symbolizes them in some way. Sometimes this is the best we can do. And sometimes this is a lot. Bud Welch, for instance, has not forgiven Timothy McVeigh, the person responsible for the death of his twenty-three-year-old daughter Julie, a Spanish translator for the Social Security Administration. But he has forgiven McVeigh's father.

A Roman Catholic, Welch believes that "even the souls of dastardly criminals should be saved." The Church teaches "that we should forgive, regardless," he says. Still, McVeigh "makes it very difficult," says Welch. "He is not remorseful in any way. He's in total denial. He doesn't give a damn. And without him asking for it, it's almost impossible. It's like trying to shower forgiveness on someone when they don't even want it. It doesn't work." So Welch is "struggling" with forgiveness, he says.

Meanwhile, Welch has received many of the benefits of forgiveness through contact with McVeigh's family. Welch first saw McVeigh's father, Bill, on television; he was working in his flower bed outside his house while a reporter asked him a question. "I don't remember the question, and I don't remember his answer, but he looked up for a second into the camera. You could see a man in deep, deep pain. I was touched by that. I thought, 'I need to talk to him. I need to tell him that I really care about how he feels.'"

A Catholic nun arranged a meeting for the two men in September 1998, three and a half years after the bombing. Welch drove from Oklahoma to upstate New York to meet Bill McVeigh at his home. Timothy's sister Jennifer joined them. First in the garden, then in the kitchen, Bud Welch and Bill McVeigh found common ground: Irish Catholicism, a family history of farming and gardening, a love of their children. "You don't just turn that love on and off," says Bud Welch. "When you think about it, you realize, Timothy is his son."

These three people, bound inextricably by the worst mass murder in U.S. history, talked for more than two hours. Welch says that he "talked about the levels of anger that I've gone through." He also told the McVeighs about Julie: her fluency in Spanish and other languages, her volunteer work with homeless people.

Jennifer talked about the local parents who had protested her hiring as a teacher and threatened to remove their children from the school because she taught there.

Timothy's high school graduation photo was posted on the refrigerator, but "there was almost no discussion about Tim," Bud recalls. When he told Bill and Jennifer McVeigh that he believes Timothy is guilty, he "did not wait for a response, because I didn't want one. I think they accept that he did it."

But Welch also told them that the murder was not their fault, and that he was not angry with them. He now calls the meeting "a spiritual experience" and says that it was "almost like forgiving, in a way, when you face them and tell them that you don't blame them for what he did. You don't blame any of the family members. You're not angry at them. That's extending the olive branch."

Welch had initiated the meeting "for very selfish reasons—just for me," he says. But afterward he realized that "it was also for them." The healing effect on Timothy's father was confirmed by the nun who had arranged the meeting. Afterward she told Welch, "Bud, I hear a spirit in Bill McVeigh's voice I haven't heard in years."

The Chinese occupation of Tibet has resulted in the deaths of 1.2 million people owing to massacre, execution, starvation, and suicide. Nevertheless, the Dalai Lama, a Nobel Peace Prize winner and the spiritual leader of Buddhists in Tibet and worldwide, refers to the Chinese as "my friends, the enemy." He tells a story of a Tibetan monk who spent eighteen years in a Chinese prison, then escaped to India. The Dalai Lama asked him what he thought was the biggest threat to him while he was in prison. What he most feared, he said, was losing his compassion for the Chinese.

The Dalai Lama says, "My true religion is kindness." He doesn't seem to limit this kindness to the people who have never disappointed him or hurt his feelings. "The sun shines for all," he says, "and makes no discrimination. This is a wonderful metaphor for compassion. It gives you a sense of its impartiality and all-embracing nature."[7]

He's not advocating compassion only for people you understand, or only for those who commit minor crimes. Compassion for the people you already like is easy. "If you do not practice compassion toward your enemy, then toward whom can you practice it?" asks a Mahayana Buddhist text.[8]

Jesus says something similar in the Bible.

What I tell you is this: Love your enemies and pray for your persecutors. If you love only those who love you, what reward can you expect? Even the tax collectors do as much as that. If you greet only your brothers, what is extraordinary about that? Even the heathens do as much. There must be no limit to your goodness, as your heavenly father's goodness knows no bounds. (Matthew 5:44–48)

Judaism also counsels people to pray for their enemies. "If a man has received an injury, then even if the wrongdoer has not asked his forgiveness, the receiver of the injury must nevertheless ask God to show the wrongdoer compassion," instructs the Talmud.[9] If a Jew is asked to help a friend and an enemy at the same time, he is obliged to first help the enemy. There are two reasons for this: (1) to crush your own evil *yetzer* (the egocentric part of the personality that delights in others' suffering), and (2) to "crush the enemy's *yetzer*, thereby enabling him or her to want to become a friend."[10]

The author Henry James, asked by his nephew for some guidance, said, "Three things in human life are important. The first is to be kind.

The second is to be kind. And the third is to be kind." Like the Dalai Lama, he seemed to be directing his young relative to be kind all the time, to everyone, not just to the people he didn't happen to be mad at.

Jesus also said, "Be compassionate as your Father is compassionate." Author and priest Henri Nouwen called this "perhaps the most radical statement Jesus ever made." Jesus was asking people to be as compassionate as God.

Inevitably, people do things that hurt us. Inevitably, we do things that hurt others. This is part of what it means to be human, to have feelings, to be imperfect, to be vulnerable. Compassion moves us beyond our own wounds and back into the human community. It asks the question: What sort of people do bad things? The answer: lonely, scared, ignorant, confused, sick, misguided, angry, fallible, human sort of people—in other words, all of us.

Chapter 7

HUMILITY:
"WE ARE ALL STRUGGLING"

*H*umility is what we want other people to have. We want them to admit that they were wrong and to acknowledge humbly their shortcomings. Sometimes they do, sometimes they don't. Either way, there's value in examining our own shortcomings. Sometimes this emerges in the process of seeking compassion for the person who hurt us: As we search for compassion for that person, we inevitably shine the light back on ourselves, illuminating our own flaws and failings. Ideally, we do this too with compassion. Tenderly. With understanding that to err is human, and that we are human ourselves. Naturally, we encounter some resistance from our smug, self-righteous ego: "Mistakes? Moi? I've never done anything like. . . ." Yet ultimately, we can feel relief as we step down from the morally superior pedestal and rejoin the human race.

For me, humility emerged when I least expected it, as I was exploring the issue of reparations. Bruce had betrayed me, and harmed me, and never paid for it, neither monetarily nor by serving prison time or doing community service. The statute of limitations had long since expired, so I had no legal right to sue him, but as I searched for a way to find peace with him, I began to wonder: Should I ask him for some sort of reparations? Might it help restore balance or promote healing if he agreed to an out-of-court financial settlement? Like many people who feel victimized and angry, I wanted my perpetrator to pay.

But if monetary reparations were appropriate, I wondered, what should the amount be? How can you measure such a thing? I had already asked him to pay for our upcoming therapy session: a $220 double-hour. He had agreed. But that was a modest sum compared to the settlement a child abuser might pay if he lost a civil suit, and a modest sum compared to the amount I've paid other therapists over the years. Should I ask Bruce to finance my past or future therapy? I couldn't honestly blame all of my problems on him, but should I ask for some percentage? Maybe Bruce should pay for "pain and suffering," as they say in legal cases. But how could I calculate that amount?

What if I asked Bruce for money and he said no? Would that interfere with my forgiveness process?

What if he said yes? If the sum were larger than therapy fees, what would I do with it? Save it, in case I had an emotional breakdown that interfered with my work or required treatment? Spend it on luxuries? Donate it to a sexual abuse prevention program? Should I simply ask Bruce to donate directly to such a program?

As I wondered about these things aloud, one friend argued, "If he had wrecked your car, you wouldn't even think about forgiving him until he had paid for fixing the car, right? Don't you value yourself as much as a car?" Her analogy made sense, in a way, but I still couldn't translate the "damages" into financial terms. Though I knew of victims who had received financial settlements and reached a sense of resolution that way, I couldn't help but notice that my friend who compared me to a car was embroiled in a bitter battle with her own family, from whom she had demanded $100,000 as reparations for her father's incest and her mother's complicity. Her parents neither paid her a dime nor spoke to her again, and she remains enraged.

What finally persuaded me not to ask Bruce for money was this question, which occurred to me suddenly and jarred me: Who might someday make the same demand of me? How many people are still angry, upset, or damaged by my irresponsible behavior, sexual or otherwise?

I remember where I was when I made that shift in my attention, from Bruce's behavior to my own. I was swimming. I was halfway down the pool, halfway through a stroke. My right arm was in the air, elbow bent.

I'm a perpetrator too, I thought, stunned. I almost didn't finish the stroke. I almost didn't finish the lap. Had I not been swimming with my team, with people ahead and behind, I would have planted my feet on the bottom and stood up, gasping for air. I felt arrested, literally, by this change in perception. I too was guilty.

Have I molested fourteen-year-old kids? No, thank goodness. But have I been reckless, unkind, thoughtless, selfish, insensitive, and cruel? Yes. I have committed acts that might have made people as angry at me as I have been at Bruce. I have betrayed people who loved me. I have betrayed my own heart, failing to live up to my own standards. Some people, I suspect, are still angry with me, have not forgiven me, and believe I owe them something—an apology or an explanation at least. What if they tried to quantify how much I hurt them and demanded money from me? Should I ask Bruce for enough to cover those projected expenses?

I could try to blame Bruce for my own misbehavior. I could explain it this way: Because my boundaries were violated at an early age, I grew up confused about sex, love, romance, and exploitation and as a result made many mistakes with other people. I could contend that these mistakes were his fault, traceable to Bruce's early violation. This is an appealing but facile explanation. As an adult, I must take responsibility for my behavior.

It is not pleasant to remember my own questionable encounters, my irresponsible actions, the hurt feelings and broken hearts I've left in my wake as I sailed along, oblivious. How much easier it was to focus on Bruce's faults! Yet this inward reflection helped me turn away from victimhood and toward forgiveness. Suddenly Bruce looked different. More human. More like me.

Just because the perpetrator behaved badly doesn't mean the victim is good. Yet we tend to act like that, like innocent victims, while all around us other people hurt us. They forget our birthdays, leave dirty socks on our floors, betray our confidence, keep us waiting, make unkind remarks, steal our money, and worse. "We remain all the time against one another, grinding one another down. . . . Each considers himself right and excuses himself . . . all the while keeping none of the Commandments, yet expecting his neighbor to keep the lot!" So said Dorotheus of Gaza, a sixth-century Egyptian monk.[1]

From a more modern perspective, Alcoholics Anonymous literature explains how people use anger and blame to avoid looking at themselves.

> The moment we ponder a twisted or broken relationship with another person, our emotions go on the defensive. To escape looking at the wrongs we have done another, we resentfully focus on the wrong he has done us. This is especially true if he has, in fact, behaved badly at all. Triumphantly we seize upon his misbehavior as the perfect excuse for minimizing or forgetting our own.[2]

At least I don't molest kids. At least I'm not as pushy as that woman on the airplane. At least I've never. . . . Such rationalizations separate us from behaviors we abhor: jealousy, greed, rage, pettiness, selfishness, insensitivity, abuse. *Okay, I'm not perfect, but at least I would never do that. I'm better.*

This was a theme with people I interviewed who were stuck in nonforgiveness. "Well, sure, but at least I don't. . . ." We say, "At least I don't . . . ," when we're beginning to see what we have in common with the other person and don't want to. By then it's a desperate scramble to stay separate and above. It's not effective in the long term. And it's lonely at this "top."

But no wonder we resist. It can be disorienting. A glimpse of humility, just when we'd embraced the victim role, is like a strong unpleasant odor: pervasive and unavoidable. It can change how we look at ourselves and how we look at others. Maybe we weren't only victimized but actually participated somehow, in that offense or others. Maybe we can't forgive her for what she did to us on Monday, but she can't forgive us for what we did to her on Sunday.

It's so much easier to criticize others, overlooking our own flaws. Self-righteousness can feel good. I'd much rather go to bed mad at someone else than try to sleep with myself when I'm the one who has done something wrong.

So why seek humility? Why think about our own transgressions when it's so much more palatable to focus on those of the perpetrator, the really bad one, the one who's so much worse than we could ever be?

Here's the payoff: Anger subsides. You feel less victimized. You feel more honest, more balanced. You feel less separate from other people.

The ancient Sufi poet Kabir wrote,

We are all struggling, none of us has gone far.
Let your arrogance go, and look around inside.[3]

When we let our arrogance go and look around inside, we see that it's not true that they are wrong and cruel and hurtful and we are not. It might seem true when we're still smarting from some offense, but it's really not. Humility offers this piece of forgiveness: We're all in this together. We all make mistakes. We all have ugly parts of ourselves. I'm no better than you, and I'm no worse than you.

I find comfort in that.

As I write about each of these five keys to forgiveness and freedom, I find myself wanting to say that each is the most important one. Awareness is most important because if you don't know whom you're forgiving, and what you're forgiving them for, how can you forgive? Validation seems most important because we're social creatures who need others to acknowledge our pain. "If only he knew how much he hurt me," people lament, "then I might forgive." But compassion seems most important too: It escorts us out of our self-centered homes and reminds us that there are other people in the neighborhood who are also hurting. And now I want to contend that of the five keys to forgiveness and freedom, humility, a close cousin of compassion, is the most important—maybe because it's so important to me. I frequently suffer from feeling critical of and superior to other human beings, as if I'm an angel floating up above, shaking my finger at all those pathetic losers below. It's humility that yanks me back down to earth with everyone else, out of that awful, aloof, judgmental, and distant place.

* * *

Humility comes easiest if we have committed the exact same offense as the person who offended us. Even then, there will be times when we'll try to justify our own behavior with, "It really wasn't as bad," or, "The circumstances were different," or, "She did it to me first," or, "I had a good reason, and she didn't." But identical faults come in handy.

Mike's wife, Melissa, had an affair a few years into their marriage. As Mike struggled to forgive her several years later, I asked him whether he had ever had an affair himself. He said no, but added that before he met his wife, while he was dating, he "might have dated other people without everyone knowing." Searching his memory, he also admitted that in high school he had "stolen" his best friend's girlfriend, thus breaking the bond with his best friend. "That was different," Mike said, "because I hadn't made any vows with my best friend. But on the other hand, of course, my friend felt betrayed by me, so I guess in that way it was sort of similar to an affair."

Mike seemed to be almost wishing that he could find an affair-like offense in his own history, because he wanted to forgive and would have welcomed the sense of common frailty, the relief that comes from knowing you're not superior and hence not so far away. "It would have been easier," he admitted.

One of Ann Landers's readers wrote to say that her husband had had an affair—but so had she. Rather than act indignant when she found out about his affair, she promptly admitted that she too had been sleeping around. "We agreed to forgive each other and find out what was missing in our marriage and fix it," she said. "Our marriage is now stronger than ever because of our honesty and willingness to forgive, and we are grateful to have gotten through this together." I doubt if that process was easy, but surely it was easier than it might otherwise have been had only one of them strayed.

Usually it's not that symmetrical. But if you're willing to think less literally, balance can be achieved in almost any dyad: You're human, I'm human; we both suffer and stumble and hurt other people and hurt ourselves. Another woman told Ann Landers that her "scatterbrained" husband loses his keys, wallet, and checkbook. He's also a slob, she said, who spills, drops, tears, or mangles "any item he touches." But she didn't write to complain about him. She continued, "I am organized and neat and never misplace anything, but I am also bad-tempered, inflexible, demanding, and a perfectionist. I hardly ever relax." Her husband, she acknowledged, is "easygoing, laid back, and not easily upset." She concluded with this rhetorical question: "Who really has it roughest at our house?"

We all err. We all have habits that can get on the nerves of other people. Virtually all of us break the law, whether by speeding or cheating on taxes or walking off with our employer's office supplies. Which is not to say that pocketing paper clips is equivalent to breaking into someone's house, gagging the occupants, and walking out with the jewelry. But equivalence is not the point. Common ground is the point: We are all struggling. None of us has gone far.

What about when a parent says, "Well, he murdered my son, and I've certainly never murdered anyone"?

I posed this question to Cheri Huber. Her response: "But don't many of us want to murder the murderers—either with our bare hands or through the state-sanctioned death penalty? Isn't the impulse to kill the same?

"If I were that parent," she continued, "I would do in a minute what he did to my son. But I would feel justified. I would think: 'He's just an animal, but this is revenge.'" Despite this human tendency to try to justify our actions, she says, "the real spiritual gift and opportunity in these sorts of situations is to see how I am the same way I judge other people for being."

I then approached Bud Welch, for whom my question was not theoretical: His daughter was killed in the Oklahoma City bombing. "Have you ever wanted to murder anyone?" I asked. Welch readily admitted that in the month or so after his daughter's murder he "would have become a murderer" himself if he had had access to Timothy McVeigh. At the very least, Welch "wanted him to fry without a trial."

Commonality is what we crave when we're caught doing something we shouldn't do. "I'm not the only one," we say, or, "Well, what about you?" It's what Mike Tyson did when listing the offenses of other professional athletes who have choked their coaches and spit on umpires. It's natural to seek compassion from others by trying to get the other person to admit that they too misbehave. It's harder to offer that compassion to ourselves.

The Irish journalist Nuala O'Faolain felt painfully judgmental of her mother and father for their alcoholism, for her father's infidelity, and for their "pathetic" marriage. Then one day in church she had an epiphany: "But I'd do the same myself! I'd make the choices [they] did! There's nothing I wouldn't stop at in the pursuit of even a parody of love." She told herself, "Forgive them, the same way you forgive yourself, for the same reasons you forgive yourself." At that point, she writes in her memoir *Are You Somebody?*, "something inside me, that had been agitated for as long as I could remember, went quiet for the first time. . . . Why didn't I see that before? They were only ordinary, too."[4]

When I was in high school, a friend named Guy drove me to a convenience store. As we pulled into the parking lot, we saw another car back out quickly, then swerve sharply left, ramming into a lamppost bordering the lot. Guy immediately parked our car and walked over to the driver. He wasn't hurt, just embarrassed. Guy told him, "Hey, man, don't feel bad. I've done the same thing myself."

Later I asked Guy innocently, "Have you really smashed your own car like that?"

"Oh, no," he said. "I just wanted him to feel better."

This was an early lesson for me in the use of humility, albeit in this case false humility, as a generous, compassionate gesture. Guy nudged the driver toward self-forgiveness by reminding him that everyone makes mistakes.

Humility also helped Fran, a recently divorced mother, forgive her ex-husband. "My husband had affairs and treated me horribly," she says. After the divorce, friends expected Fran to stay angry. She didn't. "I've got a five-year-old, and I didn't want to be bitter throughout my son's childhood," she says. "I realized that the way to avoid bitterness was through forgiveness. And that the way to forgive was to look at my ex-husband's behavior more compassionately, and also to take a good hard look at my own. It's not my ex-husband's fault that I married the wrong man."

It can be difficult, when facing our own transgressions, to find the line between humility and self-hate. Huber calls for a "compassionate self-scrutiny" that leads to awareness of our own shortcomings. Such gentle introspection not only helps balance the scales between our own faults and those of others but can yield useful information about who we are and why we behave as we do. The object is not to turn our anger inward, blaming ourselves or using our mistakes like whips to self-flagellate. Instead, the goal is to find our common bonds with other human beings, forgive them for their mistakes, and ultimately offer that same forgiveness to ourselves.

A Buddhist community was in turmoil because the teacher had become sexually involved with a student during a supposedly celibate retreat. At a series of meetings, other students expressed anger and confusion. "We were trying to understand how this had happened, and what we needed to do about it," recalls author Jack Kornfield.

> But these important questions were often asked with a tone of outrage and indignation. Then in the middle of one of the most difficult community meetings, one man stood up and asked a question of the group in a tone of great kindness. "Who among us in this room," he asked, "has not made an idiot of himself or herself in relation to sexuality?" The room broke into smiles as everyone realized we were all in it together. It was at that point that we began to let go of some of the blame and look for a wise and compassionate response to everyone concerned with this painful circumstance.[5]

Kornfield elaborates:

> Forgiveness does not condone the behavior of students, community members, or teachers who have caused suffering, nor does it mean that we will not openly tell the truth and take strong action to prevent future abuse. In the end, forgiveness simply says that we will not put someone out of our hearts. . . . We recognize that we have all been wronged and we have all caused suffering to others. No one is exempt. When we look into our hearts and we see what we cannot forgive, we also see how we believe the person who was wrong is different from us. But is their confusion, fear, pain really different from ours?[6]

Similarly, Jesus held up a mirror to those who wanted to accuse others, insisting that they deal with their own shortcomings first. "Let him who is without sin among you be the first to throw a stone at her" is one of the most famous of his admonitions, delivered when facing an angry crowd that was preparing to stone an adulterous woman (John 8:7).

My favorite among Jesus's comments on humility is this: "Why do you see the speck that is in your brother's eye, but do not notice the log that is in your own eye? Or how can you say to your brother, 'Let me take the speck out of your eye' when there is a log in your own eye? You hypocrite, first take the log out of your own eye" (Matthew 7:3–5).

Why waste time venting anger at others, disapproving of their behavior, and picking at the specks in their eyes when we have more pressing problems within?

In the Lord's Prayer, humility and forgiveness seem inseparable: "Forgive us our trespasses as we forgive those who trespass against us." Our own faults are right there in the same sentence with the faults of those who hurt us. Humility (asking for God's forgiveness) is inextricably linked to generosity: forgiving others.

Jesus said that the two greatest commandments were "You shall love the Lord your God with all your heart, and with all your soul, and with all your mind," and, "You shall love your neighbor as yourself" (Matthew 22:36–40). The poet W. H. Auden added a humble and humorous twist to the second one when he wrote: "You shall love your crooked neighbor / with your crooked heart." I remember that Auden line when I catch myself feeling unforgiving toward neighbors, friends, family members, or others. I prefer it to the original biblical version, because you can love your neighbors, or try to, and still feel superior to them. When you love your crooked neighbor with your crooked heart, there's no question of difference or superiority.

Lawrence Martin Jenco spent a lot of time looking at his own crooked heart during his nineteen months in captivity in Beirut.[7] The kidnapped Catholic priest reviewed his whole life and mentally apologized to all the people he had hurt. Even in the midst of beatings, starvation, and other cruelty from his kidnappers, Jenco turned his attention inward, assessing his own shortcomings and recalling how he had hurt others.

Five of the steps in the twelve-step programs focus on humility. Step 4 requires you to take "a searching and fearless moral inventory." Step 5 is to admit "to God, to ourselves, and to another human being the exact nature of our wrongs." Step 8 asks you to make a list of everyone you've harmed and to become "willing to make amends to them all." In step 9 you make "direct amends to such people whenever possible, except when to do so would injure them or others." Step 10 would have you continue to "take personal inventory" and, when you're wrong, to promptly admit it. *The Twelve Steps and Twelve Traditions* (the "big book" of Alcoholics Anonymous) cautions that you'll prefer blaming others to taking responsibility, that you won't want to reopen these wounds, and that you'll avoid making amends to certain people. Do it anyway, the authors insist.

I once read a feminist analysis of the twelve-step programs. Noting that Alcoholics Anonymous was created by a man with men in mind, this writer argued that women need to focus less on their own wrongs and more on the wrongs that have been done to them. We're already humble enough, she said. Too humble sometimes, too ready to accept blame, even when we're not at fault. We're often victimized, yet rarely in touch with our rage about that victimization. She rewrote the twelve steps. In her step 8, rather than making a list of all the people they have harmed, women are instructed to make a list of all the people who have harmed them. Her step 9, as I recall, suggested that rather than making amends, women should confront their abusers and demand accountability.

At the time, this made sense to me. I read this analysis during a phase of my life when I was filled with anger at all sorts of things, including sexism. I shared it with some friends who were in the twelve-step program. They nodded and smiled sagely, without disagreeing—then quietly returned to their meetings.

I still think the feminist analysis was right: Women do need to acknowledge and remember the wrongs that have been done to us—as I say in my "awareness" key to freedom and forgiveness. I also think that women as well as men need more humility. We need a balance, focusing neither on our own faults alone nor exclusively on the faults of others. We need "a willingness to admit when the fault is ours, and an equal willingness to forgive when the fault is elsewhere," as the AA literature points out.[8]

Humility can come first: If I humbly remember my own shortcomings, I'm more likely to forgive you for yours. But forgiveness can also come first: Once I release you from my wrath, I've created more space to take an honest look at myself. The AA creed recommends forgiving first, without waiting for an apology or anything else from the other person. "Let's remember that alcoholics are not the only ones bedeviled by sick emotions," says *Twelve Steps and Twelve Traditions*.

> Moreover, it is usually a fact that our behavior when drinking has aggravated the defects of others. We've repeatedly strained the patience of our best friends to a snapping point, and have brought out the very worst in those who didn't think much of us to begin with. In many instances, we are really dealing with fellow sufferers, people whose woes we have increased. If we are now about to ask forgiveness for ourselves, why shouldn't we start out by forgiving them, one and all?[9]

For me, humility came first, as part of my path toward forgiveness and freedom. Memories of my own "youthful indiscretions," as politicians like to put it, shocked me into admitting to myself the many times I've been dishonest, arrogant, callous, insensitive, irresponsible. As I began to look less like an angel, Bruce began to look less like a devil.

Moreover, I realized, Bruce and I are not alone. We are all struggling. None of us has gone far. That insight led me to this fantasy: This book becomes a best-seller and, despite my pleas for privacy, readers, reviewers, and reporters all start asking, "Who's Bruce?" It becomes a national obsession, an adult version of "Where's Waldo?"

I explain that I do not want reporters to find Bruce, or to harass or even question him, because I believe he has suffered enough. I respect his privacy and wish him well. However, the curiosity continues. Finally, a press conference is called. A man comes forward, declaring, "I'm Bruce." He confesses to the crime of statutory rape. Reporters swarm around shouting questions. People who know him are shocked. Others applaud his courage. But when I watch the television coverage, I see that he's not Bruce.

The next day, someone else comes forward, saying, "I'm Bruce." For a while, people are confused and suspicious, but the second Bruce convinces people that he too sexually abused teenage girls and that he too is contrite and wants to apologize—not only to me but to the community at large. But he's not really "my" Bruce either.

The next day, another man holds another press conference, and I attend. He announces, "I'm Bruce," but this time he's not even a child molester, just someone who feels remorseful about other transgressions and wants to admit humbly to God and to the assembled reporters the exact nature of his wrongs. When he sits down, another man stands and says, "I'm Bruce too." Then another man. Then another. Then a woman. Then another woman. By the end of the day, everyone is standing, even the reporters.

I'm standing too.

Chapter 8

SELF-FORGIVENESS: "THE DAMAGE I HAVE DONE TO MYSELF FADES"

My friend Kimberly Carter once borrowed a book from a friend, then failed to return it to him. She meant to, but as a busy, working mother, she kept putting it off. When she ran into her friend in their small town, she would worry that he was going to mention the book. Over time she found herself avoiding eye contact with him, then avoiding him altogether. A year went by. She lost the book. "Eventually I just started not liking him," she admits with a self-deprecating laugh.

How typical: to distance ourselves from others, and even stop liking them, because they remind us of our own shameful actions. Fortunately, there is an alternative. If we can forgive ourselves for our mistakes, we can face our friends or colleagues or family members and make amends for any ways in which we might have hurt or disappointed them. That way, our relationships with others need not suffer, because we're addressing the core issue: our relationship with ourselves.

Self-forgiveness is the most important key to forgiveness and freedom. I said that already about the other four keys, but this one is the most important as well. We have to live with ourselves each day and sleep with (or lie awake with) ourselves each night.

If we *start* here, with self-forgiveness, we can preserve relationships that would otherwise suffer, and we can become more content with ourselves. It's like the song "Let There Be Peace on Earth . . . and Let It Begin with Me." Self-forgiveness is about "beginning with me." It's about spreading peace by treating yourself kindly. When you treat yourself with love and compassion, you become a lot kinder to everyone else.

Ending with this key also works. If we turn to the self-forgiveness key last—after awareness, validation, compassion, and humility—then self-forgiveness will probably unlock the heart's final door. I list it last because, realistically, we usually forgive ourselves only after considerable emotional or spiritual work involving other people. Often it doesn't even occur to us that there's anything to forgive ourselves for until after we've forgiven everyone else and still feel unresolved. Self-forgiveness becomes a last resort, something to try when there's no one left to blame, or forgive, but ourselves.

Forgiveness always involves a relationship. It's the generous act of welcoming an offender back into your heart. Self-forgiveness involves your relationship with yourself. It's the generous act of welcoming yourself back into your own heart. Opening the doors of your heart to yourself, for yourself. It's one of the kindest, most loving things you can do.

One day when my young friend Lianna was four years old, she was jumping on her bed and chattering about her imaginary friend Bartok the bat and her ability (which she demonstrated) to sing vibrato. I was enjoying her exuberance and her many talents but was nevertheless having a lonely sort of day, feeling left out and sorry for myself. Then, at the height of one bounce, Lianna looked me right in the eye and said, "I will love you forever."

She shocked me right out of my self-pity. When she and I both bounced back down to earth, I found myself hoping that she will indeed love me forever, although soon afterward she told me with just as much certainty that she will marry her little brother.

But her declaration led me to this thought: What if we could say that to ourselves: *I will love you forever?* What if we not only promised that to ourselves but believed it, and made good on that promise? Forever, no matter what?

People seem to crave this sort of unconditional self-forgiveness, this freedom from self-criticism and self-loathing. "I wish I could forgive myself," people tell me, or, "I'm afraid I'll never be able to forgive myself." It's something audience members ask me about when I speak on this subject: "How can I forgive myself?" They're not asking if it's possible, or if it's correct, or if there is religious precedent for it. They want guidance on how to accomplish it because they're in pain.

Yet self-forgiveness does not seem common. I don't know too many people who treat themselves gently, forgiving themselves for daily mistakes. Often we don't even realize that self-forgiveness would be useful. Instead, we berate ourselves, as if brutal self-recrimination might rectify past problems. For many of us, guilt and regret are constant companions, far more familiar than self-forgiveness or self-love.

Some of us don't offer ourselves forgiveness because we feel unworthy. We don't believe we deserve kindness and compassion, even from ourselves.

Some believe self-forgiveness would be dangerous, a license to behave badly. We're afraid we might let ourselves off the hook, granting ourselves forgiveness before we've acknowledged the problem, or taken responsibility for it, or learned anything useful from the mistake. *Self-punishment* seems more appropriate, and a better deterrent.

Some of us believe we need to leap through a series of hoops: admit to the wrongdoing, experience remorse, recognize the victim's suffering, offer restitution, pay a penalty to society, correct the wrong so it does not happen again, and make amends. All that before we can give ourselves a break.

Some object to self-forgiveness on religious grounds. Although the concept of forgiveness is a religious universal, the concept of forgiving *ourselves* does not appear in any major religious texts: Christian, Hebrew, Buddhist, Islamic, Hindu, Confucian. Many modern theologians address the concept in their teachings or writings, but some oppose it, maintaining that we can be forgiven only by God or other people, not by ourselves.

Others say we can't forgive ourselves because we can't fairly assess our own wrongdoing. We're too close to the situation; it's a conflict of interest. Like judges who must recuse themselves from cases in which they have a personal interest, we must leave the forgiveness up to others, since we can't possibly be objective.

People are also reluctant to forgive themselves because others might criticize them for it. Consider the extreme example of the mother who steps into the house to answer the phone, leaving her toddler alone in the backyard. When the little girl falls into the pool and drowns, the mother is inconsolable. But must she be inconsolable forever? What if she forgives herself? What if she offers herself compassion in response to her own agony? What if she grieves for her daughter thoroughly and deeply and also eventually allows herself to enjoy life again—swimming, chatting with friends on the telephone, playing golf on Sundays? How will her friends and family respond? Wouldn't many people be more comfortable if she continued to feel miserable for the rest of her life? People might gently urge her to forgive herself, but do they really mean that? If she finds a way not to be forever trapped by grief and guilt, won't people think she is irresponsible, or in denial, or crazy?

Perhaps it's the rarity of self-forgiveness, combined with its inherent appeal, that makes so many of us uncomfortable with it. The friends who are most judgmental of the mother whose daughter drowned, for example, probably don't know how to forgive themselves, even for mistakes with much less severe consequences. "When people forgive themselves . . . they leave the rest of us behind," notes Beverly Flanigan, a therapist specializing in forgiveness. "They reconcile their humanness and transcend it at the same time. Forgivers have found a way to peace, while the rest of us watch in confusion, anger, or envy."[1]

Yet I believe that until we forgive ourselves—for our numerous human failings—we cannot fully forgive others. As long as we are denying our own weaknesses, we will remain fixated on the weaknesses of others. As long as we are punishing ourselves, we will tend to punish others. We can't hate ourselves and love others—or love ourselves and hate others.

I think there's too much self-flagellation, too much endless self-loathing. I don't think people need more self-punishment. I think they need more self-compassion. The very question *How can I forgive myself?* indicates that you have already been punished.

But doesn't self-forgiveness grant license to keep misbehaving? No. Denial does that. The self-forgiver must become aware of what happened, then find compassion for the person who is hurting: the self. Through this honest assessment and warm self-embrace, she becomes free from the shame of the past so that she can choose to act differently in the future. Self-forgiveness means offering ourselves the same gentle acceptance and love we want from others. Those who feel loved and accepted are much more likely to do the right thing than those who are filled with self-hate.

When we forgive ourselves, we learn how forgiving happens. We get better at it. This information is then useful when we're confronted with the possibility of forgiving others.

I find that there are lots of opportunities to practice forgiveness right here within myself because I'm the one whose mistakes are always bothering me. I annoy myself much more than other people annoy me. When I focus on forgiving myself, I don't have to wonder about another person's motivation, or whether they're truly sorry, or what our future might hold. It's all here in one package: the offense, the regret, the apology, the contrition, and, when things are going well, the forgiveness. Then, when I feel forgiven, I'm much more capable of loving and feeling compassion for others, and forgiving them. The doors of my heart are already wide open.

I can think of three situations that call for self-forgiveness: when we have hurt someone else; when we have hurt ourselves; and when we have hurt no one but feel guilty anyway. The first situation—when we have intentionally or unintentionally injured other people, especially people we love—is generally the most difficult. We have then created two problems: We have damaged our relationship with the other person, and we have damaged our relationship with ourselves.

Assuming we have a conscience and have noticed the injury to the other person, we might have violated our own sense of decency; we might have failed to meet our own ethical standards for moral, helpful, or kind behavior; or we might have shamed or embarrassed ourselves. If we don't acknowledge our failures and forgive ourselves for our mistakes, our guilt or embarrassment is likely to even further damage our relationship with the person we hurt.

Often, in our hunger for self-forgiveness, we try to get the other person to do our work for us. We might talk with that person, offering an apology or an explanation or a promise not to do it again, and listening to their feelings or concerns, hoping they'll forgive us, thus making it easier to forgive ourselves. Unfortunately, they often don't give us what we want, at least not immediately.

If the one we hurt is gone—if, for instance, we euthanize a pet, then have second thoughts about it, as I have done—our lack of self-forgiveness can threaten to ruin our relationship with ourselves as we torture ourselves with doubts or criticism.

When, in the second situation calling for self-forgiveness, we have hurt or embarrassed or disappointed ourselves, we become both perpetrator and victim of our own mistake, transgression, or moral lapse. In this case, we're the only person for whom forgiveness is a possibility because we're the only person involved. Many of us are crueler, and more hateful, to ourselves than we would ever be to someone else. "The damage we do to others is nothing compared to the damage we do to ourselves," says the Talmud.

Sometimes we're tempted to blame others anyway. The business owner and former workaholic Diana says she used to blame her husband for making her work so hard. "I used to hate him," she says, "and I've told him that—how much I used to hate him. Now I realize that I was just angry because I was working so hard it was killing me. I was actually angry with myself."

In the process of forgiving herself, she says, her marriage improved.

"Did he change too?" I ask.

"No," she says with a laugh, "but instead of always focusing on what he doesn't do, I now recognize him for what he does do. We have a beautiful home, and he's the one who cares for it. He's a steadying force. Some people give roots, some give wings. He gave our children roots."

It's so much easier to blame other people, even for our most personal failures. Late to a meeting, we want to blame the traffic, or the snow, or the fact that someone gave us poor directions. Unfortunately, with this type of transgression, it's usually our own fault: for not double-checking the directions, for not reading the map carefully, for not embarking on the journey sooner. There is no one else to blame, and no one else to grant forgiveness. It's the quintessential inside job.

The third situation that calls for self-forgiveness is when we have done nothing wrong but feel ashamed or guilty anyway. Self-forgiveness can seem moot. If you did nothing wrong, you have nothing to forgive, right? But people often feel guilty for things that are entirely beyond their control: for being young, for being innocent, for being in the wrong place, for being unable to protect themselves, for not having magically protected someone else. Relatives of people who commit suicide often feel guilty for not having prevented it. Rape victims often feel guilty for having worn the wrong clothing, or having gotten drunk, or having attended a wild party, or having failed to fight off a man. While your sense of responsibility may be inflated and irrational, the need for self-forgiveness is real.

This was the case with me regarding Bruce. I was a minor. I was four-teen when the exploitation began. I know now that it was not adultery, as I thought then. Nevertheless, I had to forgive myself for being naive, for lying to my parents, for trusting someone who was not trustworthy, and for not stopping it.

Megan, the mother of the Texas teenager who was struck by a drunk driver while riding his bike along a highway shoulder, struggled with irra-tional self-blame following her son's death. "I blamed myself for letting my son buy that bicycle," she told me. "I blamed myself for allowing my son to push his curfew later that Friday evening. I blamed myself for not having a car to bring my son home in that night. Geez, I blamed myself for everything you can possibly think of and more." Eventually, she real-ized that "nothing that I did or didn't do mattered. I didn't kill my son. A drunk driver did." Nevertheless, she felt a need to forgive herself for not having miraculously saved her son. She discovered this self-forgiveness, she says, through Jesus's teachings, and through his forgiveness of her sins.

For Megan and many other religious people, self-forgiveness is intri-cately connected to God. Sometimes, as in Megan's case, a sense of God's unconditional forgiveness helps people forgive themselves.

Other times, it is in their efforts to forgive God that people learn to forgive themselves. Debbie Morris, author of *Forgiving the Dead Man Walking,* explains this dynamic. Angry at God for allowing her abduction and rape to happen, she realized that in order to forgive God she needed to experience his forgiveness. So,

> over a period of weeks, whenever I remembered something I'd done wrong, or something I hadn't done right, I simply prayed and asked God's forgiveness. . . . As I did this, an incredible thing happened. As I came to know and feel God's forgiveness, it was suddenly easy to forgive myself. If God who is holy and perfect could forgive me, who was I to think I should hold myself to a higher standard? If he didn't blame me, neither could I! What a new and incredible sense of freedom![2]

It doesn't matter if our pain seems trivial to others, or incomprehensible, or irrational. When considering our ability to experience joy and love and hope on a daily basis, it doesn't really matter if others forgive us, or even if God forgives us. The real question is: Can we forgive ourselves? The Buddhist teacher Sogyal Rinpoche says, "To the man who cried out, 'Do you think God will ever forgive me for my sins?' I would say, 'God has already forgiven you, for God is forgiveness itself. To err is human, to forgive, divine. But can you truly forgive yourself? That is the real question.'"[3]

A few years ago I struggled with self-forgiveness—which is to say, I struggled with self-recrimination, self-blame, and self-doubt—after I euthanized Kabir, a loyal companion of mixed German shepherd descent who had been my best friend for twelve years. A stray, he arrived on my doorstep one day and never left. Indoors, his soft footsteps followed me from room to room. Outdoors, without a leash, he stayed by my side.

When neighbors stopped me to say, "He's so quiet!" "So dignified!" Kabir would just sit and stare up at me adoringly. One time a businessman, dressed in a suit, hurrying toward a meeting, slowed, stopped, then bent down and kissed Kabir on top of his head. Kabir evoked that kind of tenderness. So his death broke my heart, and I grieved for him the way I would grieve for a family member. But what I suffered over even more, and had trouble forgiving myself for, was the euthanasia process.

In his final three weeks, Kabir had lost his vitality, his appetite, his bladder control. His favorite things—retrieving balls, taking walks, eating—no longer interested him. About fifteen years old by then, he was terminally ill with liver cancer. Euthanasia seemed like the most loving thing to do.

The vet was kind and competent, but something went wrong and the syringe hurt Kabir, or distressed him. From a prone, relaxed, and weakened position, he suddenly sat up, turned his head, and opened his mouth, as if to bite the vet. He never would have bitten anyone. He was the gentlest creature. Calm too. So what was the matter? An intravenous line had already been inserted in his paw. The vet held his paw to insert the needle. Kabir never liked having his paws touched. His distress might have indicated no more than that: annoyance at having his paw gripped by a stranger's hand.

But afterward it worried me. Euthanasia is supposed to be painless. Kabir had been so relaxed before that as I brushed him and read his namesake's poetry to him during an impromptu good-bye ceremony. The whole point of choosing euthanasia was to prevent him from suffering needlessly. When the vet explained her procedure, I had asked, "Don't you use a sedative?" I was remembering Kimberly's German shepherd, Tonya, who had been given a sedative.

"Kabir's already sedate," the vet explained, and I couldn't argue with that. But she struggled as she maneuvered the syringe into the catheter. That's when Kabir lifted his head in protest.

"Should I . . . ?" I said, helpless.

Finally Kabir slowly laid his head back down.

"They don't close their eyes," the vet explained. Her own eyes were teary. She drew a stethoscope out of her pocket and listened to his chest.

"Tell me," I insisted.

"There's no heartbeat," she said.

"Bring him back!"

I didn't scream that, but wanted to.

Right before Kabir's death, my friend Jean told me that she had waited too long before putting her dog to sleep. Already too weak to walk, the dog had to be carried into the vet's office. "I've never forgiven myself for that," Jean told me. "She shouldn't have had to suffer."

So the timing of Kabir's euthanasia had seemed right, not too late. But in hindsight I wondered: *Had it been too soon?*

And should I have ended his life at all? I escort spiders outside rather than squash them. I'm a vegetarian because I don't want to kill animals. Yet I had killed the animal who, for more than a decade, had been my most devoted friend.

Neighbors asked, "Will you get another dog?"

"I never really thought of Kabir as a dog," I said.

In my grief, I functioned—writing, cooking, washing my clothes. Then, in all the private, in-between times, I fell apart. I had lost my best friend. Moreover, I'd killed him. This is how I tortured myself. I replayed the death scene: the lifted head, the open mouth. What went wrong? I should have insisted on a sedative. Kabir had died in pain.

Friends comforted me. "He didn't whimper. And any discomfort didn't last long. He knew you were there, petting him. He trusted you. He was dignified, at peace."

But it was too soon!

"It wasn't too soon for him," said one friend. "It was only too soon for you."

The poet Kabir wrote:

The blue sky opens out farther and farther,
The daily sense of failure goes away,
The damage I have done to myself fades . . .[4]

Gradually, over time, things changed. The blue sky opened out farther and farther. My daily sense of failure went away. The damage I had done to myself faded.

Sometimes self-forgiveness happens this way: with time. Looking back on it, I can see that I also used the first four keys to freedom: awareness (an honest look at what happened, and how I felt about it); validation (talking to friends about my remorse and doubt and second thoughts); compassion (I indulged myself in a long grieving process, including lots of self-compassion for my loss and for the ways I was agonizing about my role in Kabir's death); and humility—after a while it occurred to me that my role in his death was actually quite minuscule. A terminal cancer patient, he had been expected to die in the next few days with me or without me. I hadn't really controlled his death much more than I'd controlled his birth or his appearance on my doorstep. He lived a long life, and throughout I took care of him as well as I could. That was all I could do.

This insight helped too: Kabir himself would have forgiven me for any mistakes I might have made related to the euthanasia, as he had always forgiven me, whether for leaving him home alone or imposing a bath on him or not allowing him to lounge on the furniture. I saw a bumper sticker that summed up this marvelous truth: "To err is human, to forgive, canine."

We can't all be as good as dogs. Their ability to forgive us (and apparently themselves) sets too high a standard for most of us to reach. However, I offer this advice anyway: Forgive yourself instantly, or readily, or as soon as humanly possible. Whether you've hurt yourself or hurt someone else or hurt no one, forgive yourself first.

This is something I learned on the basketball court, and it has become for me a mantra: Forgive yourself immediately for all mistakes. During a basketball game, everyone makes mistakes. Turnovers, missed shots, and fouls are part of the game. Remember that kid in junior high who ran the wrong direction and scored in the other team's basket? Some errors are worse than others, but basketball teaches you to forgive yourself. Maybe you steal a ball and dribble furiously, the basket just ahead, like a promise. But something goes wrong, and you bounce the ball too hard off the glass. It ricochets into the eager hands of an opponent. The crowd groans. You might want to hang your head in shame, but you can't. There's no time. Nor can you chase after your teammates and beg their forgiveness. You have to sprint back down court and play good defense. That's all. If you don't do that, you're making two mistakes. Basketball is like that: very swift.

Life is like that too. It flies by quickly, and for every moment you spend regretting what happened or punishing yourself for your mistakes, you're missing the next present moment. You can *learn* from mistakes, but there's no time to get mad at yourself about them. You have to sprint back down court, ready for life's next adventure, whatever that may be.

Imagine that a husband cruelly teases his wife about her weight at a dinner party. Deeply hurt, she refuses to speak to him in the car on the way home. He tries to start a fight to distract himself from the painful fact that he has acted like a jerk. She won't fight; she just cries. He's embarrassed by his behavior, ashamed of having hurt her feelings, and ashamed of his desire to exhibit, in front of his friends, a thin, young trophy wife instead of the graying, flabby, but real and beautiful person who is sitting beside him in the car, crying. Insecure and remorseful, he begs for her forgiveness. It's the only thing he can think of that might make him feel better, and he desperately wants to transcend his own pain, shame, and self-recrimination. She seems to have this thing he wants, so he asks for it: "Please forgive me." He might even get melodramatic: "I can't live with myself until you forgive me." He might not even say he's sorry first, or might not dwell on that. By focusing on obtaining forgiveness from her, he's distracting himself from the memory of his cruel words, which caused the problem in the first place.

However, she's not ready, and may never be. Certainly she's not ready now, when she's immersed in her own shame about her protruding paunch and her husband's public mocking of it. Sitting there in the car, she can barely exhale, she's so enraged and humiliated. She's in no shape to give him a gift, and it's not fair of him to place that burden on her, demanding that she give him what he needs to heal—especially right now, when she's got her own pain to deal with.

Besides, her forgiveness might not be sufficient. The husband might still feel awful about his actions. And she might never forgive him, no matter how sincerely he might apologize. All of us know this experience: offering an apology, and trying to fix a relationship, but being met with anger or silence. What then? What if she never forgives him? Must he be sentenced to perpetual remorse? And if he clings to that self-recrimination, or even self-hate, how loving can he be with his wife—or, after the divorce, with his next wife?

Self-forgiveness is a better choice. It works better than denial ("nothing bad happened") or self-hate ("I'm a bad person") or self-delusion ("I didn't do it") or rationalization ("it wasn't very bad"). It works better than begging someone else to forgive us.

Imagine what might happen if the husband could forgive himself first. He might begin by thinking about what he did and gaining some insight into why he did it (the awareness key). Maybe his father treated his mother that way. Maybe he feels insecure about his male friends' affection for him. Maybe he's angry about having just been diagnosed with arthritis. After he gains some awareness of what happened—and how it affected all the people involved—he might seek his own humanity, sympathizing with the scared or lonely or misguided man who just belittled his own lover to their friends (the compassion key). He might also remember his own protruding stomach, or his balding head, or whatever physical imperfections he has (the humility key). Then, having taken an honest look at his actions and having accepted that he is human and fallible, he could welcome himself back into his own heart.

At that point, he could approach his wife, apologize, and offer to work with her toward some resolution of the underlying tensions between them. His self-forgiveness would free him to do the right thing, regardless of her response.

At that point, his heart already open to himself, he would be more receptive to hearing about his wife's pain. He would no longer be distracted by his own guilt. He would still appreciate her forgiveness, if she chooses to offer it to him, but he wouldn't need it so much anymore.

When we forgive ourselves first, we become stronger. Our own pain is no longer the driving force behind our apology, and we no longer approach the person we have harmed as a supplicant. We become ready to support them in their pain because we're not so needy ourselves anymore. With an apology, we're now offering a gift, not making a request.

When we forgive ourselves first, we can admit things we would never admit otherwise, because we don't have to be so defensive. We can laugh at ourselves. We don't have to worry about what others' judgments might be, because we're not judging ourselves.

Recently, I said something hurtful to a new colleague in a meeting. It was a tense, difficult meeting for everyone, and afterward I was angry with myself for that one comment I'd made. I wanted to call the colleague and apologize. Why? I was worried about how she felt. But mostly I was troubled by my own regret. I wanted to call her to make *myself* feel better.

I delayed making the call, choosing to forgive myself first. It was difficult; I was really suffering. But by the time we saw each other a few days later, I had forgiven myself. At that point, I did apologize to her, and by then it was for her sake, not mine. I didn't beg for forgiveness. I didn't even ask for it. Whether she chose to forgive me or not, immediately or later, was up to her. Having already forgiven myself, I was in a much stronger, more poised, more relaxed position. I apologized sincerely but also clearly, without a dual agenda. Self-forgiveness freed me to do the right thing and to do it cleanly, without letting my own neediness get in the way of my apology.

Over time she did forgive me, apparently, and that relationship blossomed into a friendship. I wouldn't attribute the friendship to that one early experience, but I do think that all relationships improve as a result of self-forgiveness.

Katherine had to forgive herself before she could forgive her mother. It wasn't easy, because both mother and daughter seemed to believe that Katherine's offense was more egregious. It also wasn't easy because Katherine's mother never apologized for her own role in their conflict.

Katherine was nineteen when she told her parents that she was getting married. She and Bill had fallen in love when she was attending Wellesley and he was at MIT. Her parents opposed the marriage, as did his. "They thought we were too young," recalls Katherine. "My mother even talked to his mother, trying to call it off." Katherine and Bill married anyway, without inviting either set of parents to the wedding.

"I was playing out the child-of-the-sixties thing," says Katherine, now an associate professor at an east-coast university. Not being invited to the wedding "was the kind of thing parents are supposed to be hurt by, but get over."

Katherine's mother never got over it, however, and refused to speak to Katherine for four years. When Katherine visited, her mother would leave the house.

"It was awful," recalls Katherine. "It was debilitating. I have four younger brothers, and I missed four years of their growing up. I was hurt, but I tried to act normal, sending cheerful letters home. Later I learned that she threw the letters away unopened."

A couple of years after the wedding, Katherine's mother developed a brain tumor, and Katherine told her father that she wanted to fly home for her mother's surgery. "You can't come here," he commanded. "She doesn't want you here."

The tumor turned out to be benign, but the pain of the mother's rejection seemed to be metastasizing to all members of their extended family. The turning point came when Katherine attended a Thanksgiving dinner at her paternal grandmother's house in 1973, four years after the wedding. About forty relatives were there—but not her mother. "That day, with my mother not there for the gazillionth time, and with everyone dancing around that fact, finally I'd had enough," recalls Katherine.

She left the gathering and drove to her family's house. It was empty, but Katherine looked at her mother's calendar and found that she had a tennis date with a friend. Katherine called that friend, Betty, who said that the game had just ended and her mother was on her way home. Realizing that Katherine was in the house, Betty said: "Oh, my God, get out of there. She'll get a knife."

"This was my mother's good friend, telling me that my mother was going to hurt me," says Katherine, still disbelieving. "I remember saying something like, 'Well, I'll try to keep her away from the knives.'"

When her mother walked in the back door, Katherine was sitting at the kitchen table. "She saw me and went right upstairs, right past me, without speaking," says Katherine, who followed her mother halfway up the staircase, then called out, "I'm not leaving until you and I talk."

They talked. Katherine told her that their feud was "hurting everybody else in the family" and demanded a rapprochement. Her mother listened. "It was very awkward," Katherine recalls. "She didn't stab me, but I didn't leave with warm feelings."

The two did spend time together after that, joining other family members on a trip to Europe aboard the *Queen Elizabeth 2,* a vacation Katherine remembers as "very tense. We squabbled a lot." When her mother was diagnosed with colon cancer several years later, Katherine was present for the surgery and some subsequent chemotherapy sessions. When her mother fell into a coma at the end of her life, Katherine sat in her hotel room, knitting an "incredibly long, complex cable-knit blanket" that she never finished.

The two never reconciled, "and I don't think she ever forgave me," says Katherine. But Katherine forgave herself, which enabled her to forgive her mother for her "prolonged, irrational, and punitive" response to her daughter's marriage. "As the perpetrator of the act that set her off, I felt guilty. In her worldview, I had done the bad thing, something so unforgivable that the burden would always rest on me. But if I had let it go on forever, my mother would have died without us ever speaking again. The damage would have persisted, dividing the family. So I had to overcome my feelings of being bad in order to forgive her."

She forgave herself, she explains, by remembering that she was just nineteen when she married, and by recalling her own long struggle with guilt and ostracism. By the time she confronted her mother, she was not plagued by self-hatred. She was not groveling. She just wanted the feud to stop. Despite the fact that her mother never granted her the forgiveness she wanted, Katherine feels "at peace," she says. She has been forgiven.

Sometimes we can't forgive ourselves. Sometimes our own internal critic is too loud and persistent, or our offense seems too great. Sometimes we haven't experienced enough love and compassion from others to know how to direct it inward.

The spiritual teacher Jack Kornfield cautions us not to try to force forgiveness. When we can't feel compassion for someone who hurt us, when we feel "only the burden and the anguish or anger . . . be forgiving of yourself in this as well."[5]

The same goes for an inability to forgive yourself. If you can't forgive yourself for something you've done, try forgiving yourself for that inability. If you can manage this—if you can forgive yourself for not being forgiving enough—then you are indeed engaging in the act of self-forgiveness: practicing it and offering it to the person who needs it most.

Part III

COMPLICATIONS, CLOSURE, AND BEYOND

Chapter 9

APOLOGIES AND
OTHER CONDITIONS:
"I'LL FORGIVE YOU IF . . ."

*B*ruce first apologized when I called him out of the blue to interview him for *The Stronger Women Get, the More Men Love Football*. "You don't know how badly, if I hurt you, that I want you not just to accept an apology from me, but to forgive me," he said. That initial apology was complicated by the fact that I wasn't expecting it, I hadn't really thought about what happened between us, and I had no idea what might be involved in forgiving someone for an offense of this magnitude.

Five years later, when we sat down together in his office and he said, "Mariah, I'm so sorry I hurt you," that apology was complicated by the fact that he put his hand on my arm, I did not want his hand on my arm, and I was unable to tell him to remove it.

Bruce also apologized in letters and in the therapy session. He apologized nonverbally too, through his kindness and his active listening. But for a long time, his apologies didn't seem sufficient, didn't fulfill all my demands, spoken and unspoken. For instance, I wanted Bruce to read the chapter of *The Stronger Women Get, the More Men Love Football* in which I describe my rage about his sexual abuse. He said he intended to, but when I asked him about it later, he said he did "not yet have the strength."

I also wanted Bruce to come out as a former child molester. I wanted him to speak about the issue in public and offer himself as exhibit A, explaining why he did it, why he stopped, and what toll the abuse took on everyone, including himself. I believed that, as a respected community leader, he could have had a powerful impact on other men and boys if he came forward in this way. He refused, contending that the members of his community would never accept him if they knew the truth.

My approach was rooted in the conventional wisdom that the perpetrator has to earn forgiveness by meeting certain conditions. Howard Gardner, professor of education at Harvard University, says that forgiveness is a "two-way process" that "requires acts of regret and penitence on the part of the offending person. These acts must be genuine and continuing, and not just done for the purpose of being forgiven. One earns the privilege of being forgiven by taking responsibility for one's actions."[1]

Some therapists agree: It's wrong or impossible to forgive unless certain conditions are met. Janis Abrahms Spring, author of *After the Affair: Healing the Pain and Rebuilding Trust When a Partner Has Been Unfaithful*, says, "You can't forgive those who refuse to acknowledge and redress the harm they've caused you." Without remorse and restitution from the wrongdoer, false forgiveness merely hides the wounds "under a shroud of smiles and pleasantries, and allows them to fester."[2]

In her acclaimed book *Trauma and Recovery: The Aftermath of Violence—From Domestic Abuse to Political Terror,* Judith Herman dismisses forgiveness as "out of reach for most ordinary human beings" and maintains that "true forgiveness cannot be granted until the perpetrator has sought and earned it through confession, repentance, and restitution."[3]

I disagree. I think confession, restitution, remorse, and more might be important for reconciliation in an intimate relationship. But forgiveness can happen without any action at all on the part of the wrongdoer. I didn't know this when I started dealing with Bruce. I acted as if forgiveness were a commodity to be bartered for: If you give me these things, I'll think about giving you forgiveness in return.

In addition to asking Bruce to read my book and speak out as a child molester, I placed these conditions on my forgiveness:

- I will not forgive you if you are currently molesting other girls.

- I will not forgive you if you have lied to me about how many girls you molested in the past.

Unspoken but implied were these conditions:

- I will not forgive you unless you take full responsibility.

- I will not forgive you if you violate my boundaries again—if, for instance, I ask you not to call me and you call me anyway.

- I will not forgive you if you act at all flirtatious or seductive.

- I will not forgive you if I don't trust that you are being sincere about this process.

To the extent that Bruce fulfilled my many requests, he facilitated my forgiveness. In that sense, I was lucky. Over the course of our six months of contact, he eventually listened to my pain, validated the truth of what happened, met with my therapist, apologized repeatedly, respected my boundaries, convinced me that he was probably not a current danger to girls, and took full responsibility. In these ways, he distinguished himself from most statutory rapists. Without his assistance, my process of forgiving him would have been different, slower, and lonelier.

But asking Bruce to meet my conditions was a gamble, and a surrender of my power. I was putting my potential forgiveness in his hands. If I had left it there, waiting for him to become the Perfect Apologizer, I never would have forgiven him. His apologies were not perfect; in the beginning, they were filled with rationalizations and excuses and attempts to convince me to take part of the blame. As I placed numerous conditions on my forgiveness, I told Bruce, in effect: "My ability to find resolution or peace will depend on you."

The keys to forgiveness and freedom are in our own hands. They're not in anyone else's hands. Yet that's how most of us approach potential forgiveness. We want the other person to do something first: apologize, repent, swear to behave better, whatever. To earn our forgiveness somehow. We're not wrong to want this. It just makes forgiveness more difficult, and it can make it more confusing about just who has the power to make it happen.

Complicating matters is that even the simplest apology can have multiple meanings. Here are some of the possible meanings of "I'm sorry":

- It was my fault.

- I feel terrible.

- I regret that you're hurting.

- I regret what I did.

- I regret that you caught me.

- I hope you don't punish me.

- I want you to stop feeling angry.

- I want you to forget about it.

- I don't intend to do it again.

- I want to feel better.

- I want you to feel better.

- I want you to like me.

- I was raised to say this; it's etiquette, like "please" and "thank you."

- Please forgive me.

- Please forgive me so I can forgive myself.

So when we hear "I'm sorry," we're often not sure what is meant, and how or if the apology can help us heal. Yet most of us crave apologies. It can be very satisfying to hear someone say "I'm sorry." We're so eager to have our pain validated. "An apology, under the right circumstances, those things can be quite important." That was President Clinton speaking, about a year before the Monica Lewinsky story broke. He was considering apologizing to the American descendants of slaves, something he never got around to, in part because people persuaded him that that particular apology would not be universally appreciated.

But he was right: Apologies, under the right circumstances, can be quite important. Those simple words—"I'm sorry"—can be touching, impressive, and powerful. They're touching because someone seems to care enough to try to make us feel better. They're impressive because we all know, from our own experience, how difficult it can be to admit wrongdoing.

They're powerful because they can transform relationships. The recipient usually feels less angry, more trusting, more respected. The giver usually feels less guilty and also more honorable, having chosen the moral high road.

With an apology, the offender also signals a desire "to establish or reestablish a friendly relationship," notes Jonathan Cohen, an assistant professor of law at the University of Florida. "It is a way of signaling to the injured party: 'I am your friend, not your foe.'"[4]

An apology from one mother I know transformed her relationship with her nineteen-year-old son. Craig had had trouble at school, trouble with the law, and trouble at home since he was about thirteen. By the time he was seventeen, he had been arrested ten times. Shortly after his eighteenth birthday, his mother kicked him out of the house but stayed in contact with him. During one particularly difficult month, Craig "was verbally attacking me almost daily," Julia recalls, "blaming me for all his pain and all his problems. One night he almost physically assaulted me. He was throwing things around the house and yelling, 'Fuck you!' into my face. He's a big guy. It's surprising nothing broke. I had to physically push him out the door. I was terrified and overwhelmed."

Three days later, they talked on the phone. He told her that he had driven recklessly on the way back to his apartment that night, running red lights and thinking, "What sort of asshole would treat his mother like that? Maybe I'll be better off dead. All our family problems are my fault."

Suddenly, Julia heard her own adolescent troubles echoed in his voice. "That was exactly how I felt about my family, and exactly what I used to say—that it was all my fault," she recalls. "This time, instead of arguing with him, and feeling guarded and defensive and blamed, I said, 'I'm sorry.' I was sobbing. He had been screaming at me for years, and finally I copped to it: I'm so sorry I raised a child who feels so wounded. I said 'I'm sorry' at least fifteen more times. It was not at all for effect; I was just suddenly truly, deeply sorry for all his pain, and for my part in it. It wasn't about excusing his father for his part in it, or my son for his. It wasn't self-hatred. I just heard his pain, and said 'I'm sorry.' I could hear him crying on the other end of the line. He said, 'Mom, my whole world just changed.'"

Craig drove back to Julia's house that night, and for a long time the two of them stood in the doorway, hugging and crying. Craig was wrong; his whole world didn't change. Within a week, they were fighting again. But it was a beginning. Julia's apology also felt "hugely liberating" to her, she says. "It was a gift to myself." She adds, "I do have some renewed anger at my mother for never having done that for me. My parents never apologized for anything, and I desperately wanted them to. But at least I'm changing the pattern now, with my son."

"It is the confession, not the priest, that gives us absolution," said Oscar Wilde. In other words, owning up to our misdeeds—whether through apology, penance, or confession—can itself be healing. Steve found this to be true when he confessed to his ex-girlfriend—even though she never apologized for her own part in their breakup. Steve had dated her for five years. For much of that time, she was dishonest and unfaithful, he reports. "She would say, 'Oh, by the way, I slept with my old boyfriend, but it's you I really love,'" he recalls. He would break off the relationship, then accept her back. "The old issues were never resolved. She never acknowledged that she did anything wrong, and never apologized. I would get angry, and she would turn a deaf ear."

Within three weeks of assuring Steve that they were soul mates, she announced that she was marrying someone else and wanted nothing more to do with him. Almost three years later, he is "mostly over" his devastation, he says. "We had emotional chemistry, physical chemistry, shared sense of humor—everything I'm still looking for to this day," he says mournfully. "I thought she was the perfect person for me."

He's still having trouble forgiving himself for being "a hell of a blind chump," he says angrily. "I consider myself to be observant, analytical, and cautious. I'd say I'm in the top ninety-eighth percentile of seeing through other people. I can pick up cues when they're being manipulative or deceitful. But I missed it. It's hard to forgive myself for being that blind when someone was lying to me."

However, he has moved toward self-forgiveness by apologizing to her, in detail, for his own role in their problems. In one final phone conversation, he admitted that throughout most of their relationship he had been "very critical of her in an arbitrary way—like if she was low on gas, or forgot to take the doggie bag from a restaurant. I didn't know why I did it at the time, but I now see that I had a lot of anger bottled up because of her infidelity. She had to put up with four years of that anger. So I apologized profusely for treating her badly. I remembered every little insult and apologized for every little thing. It was satisfying and cathartic, like paying my debt. I humbled myself."

He still hasn't fully forgiven his ex-girlfriend, he says, but by apologizing to her, by taking responsibility for his part in their problems, he has forgiven himself. By confessing, he has gained absolution.

An athlete named Maureen Kaila Vergara was on the receiving end of a life-changing apology. In December 1997, Maureen was in training for the year 2000 Olympics, pedaling with seven other cyclists in an Aptos, California, bike lane, when a '65 Chevrolet swerved into the pack, sent her flying through the air, then sped away. The other cyclists witnessed men inside the car laughing.

Maureen and her bike landed hard on the pavement, and her injuries were extensive: a broken shoulder, ligament damage to both knees, nerve damage, a gash on her stomach that required surgery and fifty stitches, permanent numbness, scars, disfigurement. She was able to ride a stationary bike within weeks but couldn't walk without limping for nine months.

Maureen had placed fifth in the 1996 Olympics in the points race, competing for her mother's home country of El Salvador. (Maureen is also a U.S. citizen.) After the assault, her world ranking dropped from fifth to forty-fifth. Her injuries affected not only her athletic training but also her sense of herself as a woman. "When I put on a cocktail dress, I've got a big lump on my collarbone. When I wear a bikini, I have a huge, hideous scar across my abdomen. My physical deformities are startling. If I accidentally touch my abdominal scar when I'm in the shower, it literally makes me sick."

She became afraid to ride her bike, fearful that the man who had hit her would chase her down again. A former paramedic, she had thought of herself as brave, but "for the first time I experienced a level of fear that froze me."

She obsessed about the driver, growing increasingly angry, wanting him to be caught and punished. "I felt no mercy," she recalls.

Nine months after the assault, a nineteen-year-old named Vicente Mosqueda was arrested. A suspicious neighbor had seen him spray-painting his car black. A former high school wrestling star, Mosqueda claimed they had found the wrong man. But one day before the jury trial was to start, he changed his plea to no contest on one count of felony hit-and-run with great bodily injury. The prosecution dismissed other charges of intentional assault with a deadly weapon.

Then Vicente asked for a meeting with Maureen. With their attorneys standing nearby, assailant and victim spoke to each other for the first time. "How could you drive off and leave me there like that?" she demanded. "Do you realize you've scarred and maimed my body? Do you realize you could have killed me or any of my friends? Could you have faced my mom afterward to tell her you killed me for fun?"

Vicente had tears in his eyes, Maureen reports. He said, "I would like to tell you how sorry I really am. I feel your pain inside of me. I've been living with your pain and couldn't go one more day without telling the truth."

He said he had not meant to hit her. He had not been laughing. He said he was terrified and panicked and alone when it happened. He told her he has no animosity toward cyclists now, and that in fact they frighten him.

"For over a year, I had thought of him as a monster," says Maureen. "When he faced me to apologize, I felt myself opening up, and I saw him as a human being for the first time. It was amazing to look in his eyes and to see him as a real person." It was also a relief, she adds, to hear he was not out for revenge.

Vicente expected her to yell at him—the only way he would have known how to deal with such a situation, he later told a reporter. Instead, she reached out and took his hand. "It was probably the most intense handshake I've ever had," she says. "There was so much energy. I put my hand on top of his, and he really started crying."

Maureen's parting words: "I really hope someday I'll be able to forgive you."

Even in much more trivial matters, apologies transform relationships. Deana Vaughn, a riding instructor and farm manager from Aldie, Virginia, says one of her employees walked off the job one day, abandoning the horses in his care, after arguing with a coworker about the right way to clean stalls. "It was ridiculous," recalls Deana. "They're just stalls. When we put the horses back in, they get messed up again in fifteen seconds. He blew a little thing totally out of proportion."

But that evening, after the man had walked off the job, he called Deana to apologize, admitting he had handled the situation badly. He apologized again in person the next morning, at which point Deana told him, "Okay, forget it, pretend it never happened."

But she didn't forget it. Because of his apology, the man's stature grew in her eyes. "It let me know he understood how wrong he was," she says. "Now it's even better than before because he has shown that he does understand his responsibilities and can apologize, and that makes me think more of him than if it never happened."

Six months later, she reports that her relationship with this employee is "totally fine," and that he and the coworker—to whom he also apologized—now get along too. "I think apologizing was really hard for him," she says, "and really good for him."

When an apology does not happen, and when there's no indication of remorse, forgiveness can seem impossible. Anita Hill told *USA Today* in 1998 that she has not yet forgiven Supreme Court Justice Clarence Thomas for sexually harassing her because "forgiveness ought to be deep and complete. One reason I'm not there yet is because of his [Thomas's] absolute denial that anything happened."

"Many a judge has heard a victorious plaintiff say, 'I wouldn't have minded so much if she had just said she was sorry,' or even, 'I wouldn't have taken things this far if he'd only apologized,'" Miss Manners has noted.[5]

The day the au pair Louise Woodward was released from jail, still claiming innocence in the death of eight-month-old Matthew Eappen, Matthew's mother Deborah told the *Boston Globe* that she could forgive Woodward "if only she would say, 'I did this. I'm sorry.'"[6]

Fred Goldman offered to renounce his claims to a $38 million legal settlement if O. J. Simpson would just admit that he killed Fred's son Ron and Nicole Brown Simpson. In effect, Fred Goldman said that it would be worth millions of dollars to him if O. J. would simply confess to the murder. Perhaps, along with acknowledgment, Goldman wanted an apology. Perhaps, if granted acknowledgment and apology, Goldman could forgive. Perhaps not, but on the condition that Simpson confess, Goldman was willing to forgive in the financial sense: to forgive the debt. Simpson refused, denying culpability.

Now what will Fred Goldman do? He believes O. J. Simpson killed his son. Simpson denies it. Will Fred ever forgive O. J.? Could he, in the absence of a confession? Is acknowledgment of "the truth" necessary before you can forgive?

One of the Unabomber's victims, David Gelernter, said of Theodore Kaczynski, who was convicted of killing three people and causing irreparable damage to Gelernter's hands and eye, that if it were up to him, "I would sentence him to death. And I would commute the sentence in one case only: if he repents, apologizes, and begs forgiveness of the dead men's families, and the whole world."[7] Like Fred Goldman, Gelernter was linking his forgiveness to the perpetrator's behavior.

As Clinton said, an apology, under the right circumstances, can be quite important. Here's the catch: Usually the circumstances aren't quite right. Usually, the apologizer doesn't take full responsibility. What we hear more often is, "I'm sorry, but it wasn't really my fault," or, "I'm sorry, but I'm premenstrual," or even, "I'm sorry, but I didn't do it." What then?

Twenty-year-old Jeremy Strohmeyer apologized to "every person who ever knew and loved Sherice Iverson," the seven-year-old girl he molested and killed in a Las Vegas casino bathroom. "I am truly sorry," he said in court. But the former high school honor student went on to say that he had been in a "drunken and drugged haze" during the assault and murder, and he blamed (1) Los Angeles County officials for not telling his adoptive parents about his birth mother's schizophrenia and substance abuse; (2) a former girlfriend for driving him to use speed; (3) Nevada casinos for allowing children to play at arcades; and (4) an incompetent therapist for failing to treat his problems. He also criticized a friend who was with him that night but failed to take action to save the girl.[8]

One of the most absurd apologies was issued in 1986 by Donald Manes, former president of the borough of Queens, who responded to a report that he had called New York City Mayor Edward Koch a crook: "I apologize for what was said even though I didn't say it."[9]

Tonya Harding's public apology to Nancy Kerrigan was almost as bad. Three years after Tonya admitted obstructing justice in the infamous knee-whacking incident, the two met in 1997 at the Fox studios. During their joint television appearance, Tonya said, "I want to apologize again for being in the wrong place at the wrong time around the wrong people."

Where's the responsibility in that? Being in the wrong place at the wrong time is what you say when you've had bad luck, not when you've done something wrong. Not surprisingly, Nancy did not embrace this show of noncontrition. Asked by the moderator, James Brown, "Is there room in your heart for forgiveness?" Nancy replied, "I just hope that she can learn from that and have a better life and not hurt anyone else."

Another ambivalent apology was issued by Anita, the woman who fought with her brother Rodney over his drug use and her search of his belongings. She later wrote him what she called "a letter of apology" that included the statements, "I am sorry for acting irrationally and impulsively," and, "I think we need to call a truce." Yet in that same letter, she went on to list all the things she was still angry about.

All of these examples consist of one part apology and at least one part blame. They're what I think of as "I'm sorry but" messages. Tonya Harding's message was, "I'm sorry, but I just happened to be in the wrong place." Donald Manes's was, "I'm sorry, but I didn't do it." Jeremy Strohmeyer's was, "I'm sorry, but it's everyone's fault except mine." It's what kids say when forced to apologize: "I'm sorry, but he started it." Language experts note that when *but* is used midsentence, it negates what came before. Hence, the apology is nullified by the excuse that follows.

Political and religious leaders have their own twist on this: "I'm sorry, but I wasn't even there." In the past decade, Japan, Germany, and the United States have apologized for some of their activities in World War II. The U.S. Congress has apologized to uranium miners, people contaminated by nuclear tests, people victimized by research on syphilis treatments, and native Hawaiians (for the overthrow of the Hawaii government). The Canadian government apologized to its native people. Catholic and Protestant leaders have apologized for "the sin of racism." In these examples, leaders have said, in effect, "I'm sorry *they* did that." Such an apology might have some political impact, and some usefulness, but it is very different from a personal apology: "I'm sorry I did that." No wonder people react cynically to such apologies. It's easy to apologize for things that happened before you were born. Obviously, you weren't responsible, so why not go ahead and say you're sorry?

Sometimes, instead of saying "I'm sorry," people say, "Please forgive me"—which has a very different meaning. An apology can have many meanings, but at its heart it is a statement of contrition, responsibility, and good will toward the offending party. It asks for nothing. A request for forgiveness, by contrast, is a solicitation, a plea for a gift. When Russell Henderson pleaded guilty to murdering Matthew Shepard, sparing himself a possible death sentence, he faced Shepard's parents and said he hoped "one day you will find it in your hearts to forgive me." Henderson and his friend Aaron McKinney had pretended to be gay while luring Shepard, a gay Wyoming college student, out of a bar and into their cars. The two young men then beat Shepard with a gun and left him bleeding and dying, tied to a fence post on the prairie. The jogger who found Shepard eighteen hours later thought he was a scarecrow. He died after five days in the hospital.

In sentencing Henderson to two consecutive life sentences for murder and kidnapping, Albany County District Court Judge Jeffrey Donnell said, "Quite frankly, this court does not believe that you really feel any true remorse." Indeed, Henderson had not expressed remorse; he just asked for forgiveness. Rather than telling his victim's mother how he felt about his crime, he asked her for something: a change of heart.

Matthew's mother, Judy Shepard, responded to Henderson: "My hopes for you are simple: that you never go a day without experiencing the terror, humiliation, helplessness, and hopelessness that my son felt that night."

Why is apologizing so hard? Why can't any of us say "I'm sorry" more often, more directly, with more sincerity—not for crimes committed by others one hundred years ago but for our own mistakes and oversights committed today? It's easy to imagine why murderers don't apologize more often or more easily. Someone who kills one day is unlikely to possess the courage and integrity to apologize in a forthright and responsible way the next day. But what about the rest of us? Why don't we say to our spouses and children and colleagues, "I'm sorry I hurt your feelings," or, "I'm sorry I failed to do what I promised to do"?

Sometimes people don't apologize because it's awkward. We can't be sure the other person was even hurt, and besides, we hope they don't remember. It's uncomfortable to call someone and say, "By the way, I did something really stupid (or cruel, or unethical), and I hope you didn't notice or mind, but if you did, I'm sorry." Who wants to go there?

Deborah Tannen has noted that "apology entails admitting fault. Many people see this as a sign of weakness that invites further assault." She also observes that our "argument culture" polarizes public discourse, so that every interaction involves a winner and a loser. Men sometimes avoid apologizing because they see it as putting themselves in a vulnerable, one-down, "loser" position. Status-conscious and seeking to maintain supremacy, they resist because to apologize can imply a request for forgiveness, and to request forgiveness is to risk being told no—which would mean defeat.[10]

Women, on the other hand, often apologize at the drop of a hat—when someone bumps into them on a crowded train platform, for instance. Young female basketball players are notorious for apologizing for every missed pass, every missed shot, every accidental contact—until a coach teaches them to shut up and play the game. Almost desperate to be liked and approved of, girls and women use apology to take responsibility even when it's not their fault, all in the name of keeping peace and harmony, helping everyone get along.

Confusion about who should apologize, and how, and when, begins in childhood. We teach children to say "I'm sorry" without really explaining why doing so is a good idea or what it means, and without asking them if they do indeed feel sorry. We teach them to say "I forgive you" when they don't necessarily feel forgiving. This leads to the kinds of statements that are often overheard among both children and adults: "Well, I *said* I'm sorry!"—as if that should produce automatic forgiveness.

This "should" can get in the way of both genuine forgiveness and genuine apology. The potential forgiver can feel angry and pressured if the apologizer expects automatic forgiveness, and the apologizer can feel unfairly affronted if she does not receive that forgiveness right away.

Legal issues also interfere with apologies. Lawyers often advise people not to apologize because apologies can be construed as statements of responsibility, which might lead to greater punishment. Cohen, who teaches negotiation and dispute resolution, says that an apology actually increases the likelihood that a case will be dropped, settled, or not filed in the first place. The absence of apology, by contrast, can make things worse. Often an injury is caused by an accident itself; it wasn't intentional. "There's no moral harm done by the accident itself, but not saying you're sorry becomes morally offensive," says Cohen. "Failure to apologize can be deeply disrespectful, adding insult to injury."

Yet many people won't apologize. "It's a vicious cycle," notes Cohen. "If you apologize, it might prevent a lawsuit, but you don't apologize because you're afraid of getting sued."

In fact, apologies are rarely used against defendants in court, says Cohen. Most lawyers don't even consider advocating apology, in part because apologies do not benefit lawyers, who operate in an adversarial culture in which winning, not solving problems, is the goal. If the plaintiff, satisfied by an apology, drops the suit, the lawyer gains nothing.

Over the past two decades, there has been tremendous growth in alternative forms of dispute resolution, including mediation, arbitration, and a process that's both new and ancient called restorative justice. With roots in New Zealand (among the Maori), Ontario, Canada (among the Mennonites), and the United States (among Native Americans), restorative justice defines offenses not just as crimes against the state, but as crimes against individuals, families, and communities.

Restorative justice is gaining popularity in the United States, sometimes instead of the traditional court system, sometimes in conjunction with it, and sometimes in response to minor offenses in neighborhoods and schools. Also called peace-making circles, healing circles, circle sentencing, community conferencing, family group conferencing, and community reparation boards, restorative justice takes many forms, but the process always unites and involves the victim, the perpetrator, and the community. Gathered in one room, the victim and others, including the victim's family and the perpetrator's family, speak openly about how the offense affected them. The perpetrator listens, describes the offense from his or her perspective, and, ideally, apologizes.

"After the emotions have been processed, they turn to the question, 'What does this person need to do to make amends?'" explains Kay Pranis, restorative justice planner for the Minnesota State Department of Corrections. Options include jail time, community service, financial reparations, commitments not to re-offend, and more creative solutions. Often in a criminal case, a judge must approve the sentence. If the group cannot come to consensus, the case is referred back to the court system.

"People do get sent to jail, but less often, and for less time," says Pranis. "The community goes to jail with them, in a sense. There might be a core group that will visit, or insist on certain programming. And they are aware of when [the perpetrator] will be back."

The goal is to ensure that victim, perpetrator, and community all become part of the solution. Together, everyone decides what makes sense, and together, everyone takes responsibility for restoring justice to the community.

Some restorative justice programs focus on achieving forgiveness, but "over time, people have moved away from that, because it is resented by a lot of victims," says Pranis. "They don't want to feel like they're supposed to forgive or reconcile when it's not necessarily appropriate. However, it's clear that people are trying to create conditions in which if a victim wants to forgive, it's possible. Not necessary or expected, but possible."

*   *   *

Many of our ideas about apology and other conditions related to forgiveness are traceable to Christianity and Judaism. Christianity discusses both apology and repentance but seems mostly concerned with forgiveness. Fundamental to the religion is the belief that God forgives people for their sins, and that people are required to forgive others—regardless of their feelings, the extent of the injury, or the contrition of the wrongdoer.

There is some debate about this. Some Christians interpret a famous passage in the Book of Luke to mean forgiveness must be granted only after repentance. Jesus says to his disciples: "If thy brother trespass against thee, rebuke him; and if he repent, forgive him. And if he trespass against thee seven times in a day, and seven times in a day turn again to thee, saying, 'I repent,' thou shalt forgive him" (Luke 17:3–4).

Repentance does seem to be a prerequisite here. But what if the person does not repent? Or repents only six times? Could Jesus have meant that you should not forgive them in those cases?

In the Book of Matthew (18:21–22), Peter asks Jesus, "How often should I forgive my brother if he keeps wronging me? Up to seven times?" Jesus answers, "Not just seven; seventy times seven."

In this exchange, there is no mention of repentance. In the famous "Forgive them, Father, they know not what they've done" quote, no repentance is expected or required. And in the Lord's Prayer—"forgive us our trespasses as we forgive those who trespass against us"—there is no caveat: "as long as they apologize first." It seems to me that Jesus was advocating unconditional forgiveness, with or without apology.

Judaism, by contrast, focuses on repentance. It is primarily concerned not with the forgiver but with the sinner. Rather than asking, from the forgiver's perspective, "Should I forgive?" it asks, from the sinner's perspective, "How can I be forgiven?"

Judaism holds that God directly forgives only sins against God (such as violating the Ten Commandments). God forgives us for sins against other human beings only after we have been forgiven by the people we have hurt. Judaism also stipulates that only the victims of a sin may forgive.

Judaism ritualizes apologies through Yom Kippur, the Day of Atonement. In the ten days between Rosh Hashanah and Yom Kippur, observant Jews approach those they have harmed and ask for forgiveness. The person being asked has an obligation to consider the request seriously. If that person says no, the person doing the asking must ask two more times. If, after three requests, forgiveness has still not been granted, the sinner need no longer be burdened by guilt. She or he has done what was possible to make things right and can let it go.

Suggesting that "Judaism's insights into sin, forgiveness, and atonement may be helpful to us all," the author Dennis Prager notes that "Judaism has developed a very precise understanding of what wrongdoers must do to repair themselves in the sight of God and man." To obtain forgiveness, the following conditions must be met:

1. A sinner must repent, feeling genuine regret for the deed and apologizing for it.
2. A sinner must admit that he or she has sinned, take responsibility for the sin, and not pass it off as an unintentional mistake or sickness.
3. A sinner must acknowledge a sin precisely, not just saying generally, "I have sinned."
4. The penitent must resolve "not to commit the sin again."
5. The penitent must make amends for the wrongdoing and be willing to suffer a punishment or other consequences.

"Penitence must never be cheapened by giving forgiveness to anyone who has not earned it," warns Prager.[11]

The Jewish concept of *teshuva* has also had a broad impact on how we approach forgiveness. The Hebrew word for repentance, *teshuva* is defined as turning away from evil, turning toward good, or turning toward the Torah. It's a process rather than a single act, and it reflects a changing of your ways, a new beginning.

According to the *American Heritage Dictionary,* there are two general meanings of "repent": to feel remorse, contrition, or self-reproach for what you have done or failed to do; and to make a change for the better as a result of remorse or contrition for your sins. It's the second meaning that is reflected in the concept of *teshuva.* It sets a higher standard than the first; simply feeling remorseful is not enough.

Teshuva requires going to the wronged person first, before making peace with God. "By forcing a face-to-face encounter with the aggrieved party, Jewish tradition teaches that sin is not a generalized amorphous act but something quite specific done against a particular person or group of people," writes Deborah E. Lipstadt, professor of modern Jewish and Holocaust studies at Emory University in Atlanta.

After confronting the person against whom the sin has been committed and trying to correct the wrong, one turns to God. Then one verbally confesses one's sins, expresses shame and regret for having committed this act, and resolves never to act that way again. But this does not yet bring one to the highest or most complete level of the process, *teshuva gemurah,* or complete *teshuva.* This is achieved when the individual is in the same situation in which he or she originally sinned and chooses not to repeat the same act.[12]

What a far cry from "I'm sorry"! It's more like, "I'm sorry for this particular act, and I'll never do it again, and here's a demonstration of that self-restraint." Much more than an apology, *teshuva* reflects a behavior: a turning away from evil and toward good.

Taken together, the Christian and Jewish perspectives could form a guideline for both sides of the human experience, since we find ourselves in both positions: seeking forgiveness from others, and thinking about offering forgiveness to others. It seems to me that if we followed the Christian mandate—forgive unconditionally—and also the Jewish mandate—turn toward good and away from evil—we'd have a more loving, responsible society. What often happens instead is that the sinner says to the forgiver, "I've done enough. So forgive me already." And the forgiver says to the sinner, "You didn't do enough. Repent more." In this way, the forgiver and the sinner try to control each other rather than focus on their own path toward healing.

Consider the woman who arrives late to work—again, missing a meeting. One of her colleagues thinks: *If she apologizes, I'll forgive her. If not, forget it.*

The tardy employee thinks, *Hey, I already said "I'm sorry" on my way in* (even though it was mumbled under her breath). *What do they want me to do? Get down on my knees?*

Another employee has a more compassionate response: *Surely she's embarrassed—too embarrassed to apologize.*

The employee might indeed be embarrassed, or she might be oblivious to the impact of her actions on others. Maybe she strolls into the office late on purpose, in a show of power and importance. Or maybe she's distracted and depressed about her daughter's anorexia.

Even if she does recognize the impact of her behavior on others, she might feel too ashamed or afraid to come clean. Yes, it would be easier if she would apologize—clearly, loudly enough to be heard. But if she could, she would. A lot of people can't apologize. They're incapable of it, as Sister Helen Prejean noted. The employee might be incapable of understanding why her colleagues are offended, or angry, or mistrusting. She might never agree that she did anything wrong. In fact, she might feel victimized by their confrontation and angry at them for being insensitive about her situation, whatever it may be. Behind every jerk, there's a sad story.

If her colleagues want her to explain, apologize, and promise never to do it again before they can work comfortably with her in the future, they're justified in taking that stance. The boss might reasonably demand all the same things before renewing her contract. These valid, human requests are often necessary before a relationship can be repaired. But the relationship need not be fully repaired before forgiveness can take place. Total understanding need not happen before we can forgive.

If the tardy employee asked me what to do, I would advise her to apologize. Apologies can be quite important. I would say, "Even if you had good reasons, even if you feel imposed upon, even if you don't want to—apologize."

If her colleagues asked me for advice, I would say: "Think of a time when you were too ashamed to apologize. Imagine how it must feel not to be able to apologize. Then forgive this woman, and other non-apologizers, for that inability or unwillingness. Once you forgive them for that, you've taken a step toward forgiving them for the original offense. And once you move toward forgiveness, you'll claim the ability to find peace of mind for yourself, regardless of the behavior of others."

* * *

Who apologizes? Someone who's confident enough to admit mistakes. Someone who has been apologized to. Someone who has been forgiven. Someone who forgives herself. Someone who makes mistakes, humbly admits them, then proceeds with life without undue self-torture. These people are all more likely to apologize to others.

Apologizing is a learned skill. Practiced apologizers become more fluent at it, more ready to admit mistakes and make amends. They become more humble, since they publicly acknowledge errors. They become more popular, since all of us prefer to spend time with people who are not defensive or prone to blame others for their own faults.

Effective apologies shouldn't be self-serving, like the naughty child who begrudgingly agrees to say "I'm sorry" because her teacher said she must if she wants to rejoin the group at play. This is an "I'll apologize if that will get me what I want" rather than a sincere expression of contrition. Apologies should be free, no strings attached. If the recipient of the apology feels compelled to respond with, "I forgive you," or if the apologizer becomes angry when immediate forgiveness is not granted, the apology will not have a fair chance to heal a relationship.

Don't overdo it, cautions Alcoholics Anonymous: "We needn't wallow in excessive remorse before those we have harmed, but amends . . . should always be forthright and generous."[13]

Vicente Mosqueda's seemingly forthright and generous apology changed Maureen Kaila Vergara. Shortly after they shook hands and cried together, he was sentenced to one year in the county jail and three years, suspended, in prison. "There's a huge portion of me that's forgiven him," says Maureen. This surprises her, she says. "I have been taught that to forgive is the right thing to do. Forgiveness is a mantra in my daily prayers: 'Forgive us our trespasses as we forgive those who trespass against us. . . .' I think it is easier to intellectualize forgiveness than to actually do it and mean it. I never thought I could forgive. I thought it would take something extraordinary. I didn't think it would be as simple as having eye contact and hearing an apology."

Some of Vergara's friends and family, while "incredibly supportive," don't understand her forgiveness, she says. That reaction leaves her feeling lonely. "They're still a lot harder on him. They still see him as a monster." They weren't there when Mosqueda ran into her with his car, nor when he apologized, nor when she looked into his eyes and listened to him and held his hand. "So I can't really expect them to understand where I'm coming from," she says.

Maureen's friends and family members suspect that Mosqueda "might still be covering something up," says Vergara—and she agrees with them. Witnesses saw others in the car, but he maintains he was alone. "I think he's protecting his friends," she says.

Yet when her friends point out inconsistencies in Mosqueda's testimony, or share their own theories about what's really going on, "I almost don't want to think about those things," Vergara says. "I don't want to hear it. I don't want to take back my forgiveness because it feels good."

I asked Mosqueda for an interview. I wanted to know what his apology meant to him, and what Vergara's forgiveness might mean, and if he had forgiven himself. I faxed my questions to him in jail, asking him to call me collect. The guard who delivered the fax to him called me to say that Mosqueda was going to consult with his mother before deciding about the interview. Chatting for a moment with the guard, I said hopefully, "Maybe Mosqueda's mother will encourage him to talk to me."

"Well, his mother is someone who raised a kid who drives into people for fun," replied the guard.

His cynicism and blame surprised me, and we started talking about forgiveness and apology from the perspective of a guard at a correctional institution. "I guess you've heard a lot of apologies," I said.

"These guys might actually feel bad for the moment, but that doesn't mean they're going to stop doing it," said the guard, who did not want to be named. "Usually, they don't make the connection between how bad they feel and the behavior that got them there in the first place. Or they feel bad, but not bad enough to change the behavior. They're pretty much all sociopaths. They care about themselves only."

"And the people they apologize to—are they usually fooled?" I asked.

"For a while," he said. "Then they catch on."

I wondered whether Vergara was being fooled into thinking that Vicente Mosqueda really cared about her pain. I wondered whether he was simply another selfish inmate who was saying what he needed to say to appease the people around him.

Ultimately, he declined my interview request. I didn't tell Maureen about my conversation with the guard. I didn't want to burden her with another suspicious, cynical voice, even if the guard was right. I knew that Maureen wanted to forgive, regardless of whether Vincente was telling the truth, the whole truth, or just little bits of the truth. "I know it sounds strange, but I really do want to forgive him, even if he isn't being completely honest," she told me. "Sometimes I can be too demanding of the whole truth, to my own detriment. I'm evolving, getting softer, more forgiving, less demanding that everyone be so painfully honest. I don't need to know every single gory detail. I can find forgiveness anyway."

Maureen sounded a lot like me. With Bruce, I never answered all my questions, never fully assuaged all my doubts, and never convinced him to jump through all my hoops. Eventually, I remembered that he was, as my friend Kimberly put it, "just human," and that few humans would want to "come out" as a child molester. Of course he balked at that. I also let it go that he didn't read my book as I had wanted him to. Later, in therapy, I had to let go of a few more ways that he disappointed me or didn't meet my demands. As my forgiveness process proceeded, these things became unimportant.

Ultimately, I had to forgive myself too for being so demanding in the first place. A self-critical voice inside my head was asking, *How many times must the man apologize anyway?* But it's really no wonder I began our process by saying, in effect, "I'll forgive you if. . . ." I was in pain, I needed help, he showed up, and this is how most of us think about forgiveness and talk about it—until ultimately we realize that the keys to forgiveness and freedom are not in someone else's hands but in our own.

Chapter 10

OTHER COMPLICATIONS

One time Bruce commented, "I don't know who hurts more over this, you or me." That made me angry, and I told him so. I wasn't going to let him usurp the victim role. Sexual abusers often do this, complaining about their own miserable circumstances until the victims feel sorry for them and back off. *If you're hurting, that's your own fault*, I thought. *If you hadn't molested me, you wouldn't be suffering from guilt or fear of my retaliation.*

Yet his shame and remorse were palpable, and I did feel genuinely sympathetic. I reassured him that I was not interested in revenge. I recommended therapy and followed up by asking how it was going.

Then I wondered: *Am I being too kind? Is there such a thing? Am I being manipulated? If so, how will I know?*

Human relationships are so complex. To consider forgiveness is to touch pain, grief, anger, longing, compassion, remorse. All these mixed emotions can be confusing.

Complicated histories can also be confusing. Sometimes we feel betrayed not by just one act but by several. Sometimes the other person feels betrayed too. Or neither party trusts the other. To consider forgiveness is to be reminded of how someone hurt us, and perhaps also of other people who have hurt us in similar ways, or other actions for which we have not forgiven ourselves. Myriad factors confound the straightforward question: Should we forgive or not?

While Bruce and I struggled to move forward, beyond the past, there were many ways in which we unwittingly repeated old patterns. Not only did he touch me in his office in a way I found unpleasant and confusing, but he also asked me to stop naming him in public. When he explained that he had almost lost his job, and that his family had been shattered, he was placing me in the same position he had put me in when I was a teenager: "Don't tell anyone, or I'll be terribly hurt."

I also reverted to old patterns. Sometimes I found myself wanting his approval, hoping he would express pride in my professional accomplishments, as if I were simply a returning student telling my old teacher what I'd been up to. Sometimes, talking with him on the phone, I felt inexplicably guilty, as if I were having an affair, betraying my partner. Just hearing his voice seemed to trigger that same guilty feeling that had clouded three years of my adolescence. In person, while looking at his face, feeling his touch, or smelling his scent, I unwillingly time-traveled back to those formative years when I was overwhelmed by feelings of admiration, love, and shame.

Several times I found myself wanting him to take care of me emotionally, as I had wanted him to take care of me when I was young. As I planned our therapy session, I even had a fantasy of crawling into his lap, the way a toddler might, and being cradled there. Maybe it was an old childhood desire resurfacing: to curl up in Dad's lap, to be held and comforted by him, to be soothed. Perhaps my emotional attachment to Bruce involved a transference, as psychologists call it, of my desire for nurturing from my father.

One of the most disconcerting things about my contact with Bruce was the realization that I still loved him. I probably stopped loving him for a while there, when I was busy hating him, but over time, as our new relationship deepened, my love returned. I had to check myself: *What sort of love is this? A deranged response to early abuse? An inner teenager, still crushed out on her coach? A stubborn, enduring fondness for my first love? A mature assessment of a nice guy who made some mistakes long ago? A form of gratitude for the man who was helping me heal?* I never really answered those questions, but I suspect a combination of factors contributed to my experience of loving him.

I also had to ask myself: *Am I attracted to him?*

No.

Am I still in love with him?

No.

Whew. What a relief. Even so, the love itself—my affection for him, my appreciation of him, my desire to see him, my sense that the doors of my heart were open, or opening—was unsettling. Just the fact that I had to ask myself, *Am I still in love with this person?* indicates how complex our relationship was.

He had exploited me, wreaking havoc on my ability to trust, my sense of my own boundaries, my sexuality, my integrity. Yet I had always liked this guy. I had enjoyed his sense of humor, his humility, his earnestness, and the fact that he listens well. I had thought he was my friend. Now, talking with him and even occasionally laughing with him, I remembered some of the many reasons I had loved him. He would spontaneously quote from my letters, clearly having integrated my perspective into his way of thinking. When we occasionally discussed other subjects, he was intelligent and interesting, as I had found him to be when I was young. I also respected him for being deeply religious.

I wondered about his feelings for me. *Surely he must hate me,* I thought at first, for revealing the abuse and making his personal and professional life so difficult. At one point, I even said, "You must hate me." He immediately and emphatically denied that. He seemed to appreciate the process we were going through together. He listened, answering my questions thoughtfully and, it seemed, honestly, not always saying what he might have predicted I'd want to hear. He acted very caring, even tender, yet as far as I could tell he had zero interest in me sexually, to my great relief. And he respected my emotional boundaries, giving me space when I needed it.

The depth of the feelings we shared, the kindness with which we treated each other, the sense that we were journeying somewhere together—all of it added up to an irrefutable intimacy. If I had not been a forty-year-old woman who had spent many years figuring out who she was and what love was and what sex was and what abuse was, and if I had not been already grounded in a deep, committed, long-term relationship, I might have become confused (again) about the nature of my connection to Bruce, and what we should do about it, if anything.

This is another risk of forgiveness, and another complication: in addition to anger and rage and pain, love might resurface. Then what?

Bruce and I are not the only ones who found forgiveness complicated. Rarely is it simple. Picture the grown siblings who fight at a family reunion. The argument begins when the sister asks the brother to help with the dishes. Seems a simple request, but in this family only the women wash dishes, while the men watch football in the living room. Every Christmas the sister complains about this, and every Christmas she ends up accusing the brother of "never helping." By now, "never" means "for the past thirty years," so she's got some ancient anger. But the brother has anger of his own. Why did she say, right there at the dinner table, that public schools are no good when she knows perfectly well that his kids go to public schools? Before they know it, they're arguing over why he never let her play baseball with him, and why she never took out the trash, and whether taking out the trash once a week is equal, in any sense, to doing the dishes every night. And which one of them Mom liked better.

If they're lucky, they'll do some thinking or talking or crying or even laughing about all this, and they'll sort out her pain from his insecurity and figure out that they're really mad at their parents, even though they're dead, or that they're really mad at each other but can and must forgive each other and go on.

But most siblings and lovers and longtime friends have trouble unraveling these complex tapestries—exactly who did what to whom, and who's still mad, and unforgiving, and why, and what can be done about it. Rather than work through old grievances, they let the anger accumulate and harden, like layers of rock. Most people never ask themselves: "Could I forgive my sibling (or lover, or friend) for something that happened ten or twenty years ago? Or tonight at the dinner table?" Instead, they just fight and gossip and seethe—and in the midst of all these old resentments, love each other the best they can.

When a marriage involves not only children but an affair, plus another betrayal, the prospect of forgiveness can become even more complicated.

Mike married Melissa in the summer of 1985, then entered a grueling MBA program that fall. "It wasn't the best way to begin a marriage," he admits. "I was busy all the time, not really there for her. She was lonely." Three years later, soon after their first child was born, Melissa began a yearlong affair with her supervisor. He was an older man whose job was to teach Melissa, his intern, how to become a good therapist.

Suspecting something, Mike's mother read Melissa's journal, then confronted her. "If you don't tell Mike, I will," she warned.

Mike, who had suspected nothing, found the news "earth-shattering" and immediately considered divorce. He had always viewed sexual betrayal as unforgivable: "If it happens, you can't possibly stay with that person—unless maybe if it was a onetime thing." Even before their wedding vows, Mike and Melissa had promised to confide in each other if they even grew tempted to have an affair.

But despite the fact that he was "intensely angry and intensely hurt," Mike did not leave right away because Melissa was pregnant with their second child. "There was a lot of confusion," recalls Mike. "I didn't know if the child was mine. I didn't know what the facts were, and didn't know if I could trust her to tell the truth." Melissa assured him that the child was definitely his because the affair had by then been over for a year. "It took me a while to believe that," says Mike.

Melissa said she was sorry—both for the affair and for Mike's deep hurt. To Mike, she didn't sound sorry enough. "I thought she took it too lightly. She had gotten over it, and moved beyond it, and wanted me to realize that and move beyond it also. I was nowhere near ready to do that."

Meanwhile, Mike called the other man and "raged at him," he recalls. "I'm not proud to admit this, but I told him if he ever got near my wife again, I'd kill him." Melissa was no longer working for the man at that point, but Mike reported him to his professional organization for violating its ethical standards.

The couple entered therapy immediately. It was there that the concept of forgiveness arose. "Do you still love Melissa?" asked the therapist.

"Yes, I'm pretty sure I do," said Mike.

"Can you see that Melissa is sorry?" asked the therapist.

"That took a while, but eventually I could see that," says Mike. "He didn't tell me I had to forgive, but I realized that not forgiving was going to be a burden and take a toll on us as a couple. My resentment was poisoning the relationship and also me, dragging me down. I had to get free of that."

It wasn't easy. Still overcome by "anger that would come in waves," he tried to control Melissa, demanding to know where she was each minute. "She made it clear that she couldn't live that way," he says.

After a year in therapy, Melissa grew tired of talking about the affair. "There wasn't anything more to say that hadn't been said, and she started letting me know that," says Mike. "She started saying, 'This isn't helping anymore.' I could see that the marriage wasn't going to work unless I forgave her."

In his mind, he did forgive. In his heart, he kept returning to "How could you?"

The marriage limped along. A few years later, Melissa lied to Mike about some cosmetic surgery, hiding a bill and telling him it had cost less than it did. For Mike, that was the last straw. "It confirmed that I couldn't trust her," he says. "It brought back all the pain, all the anger." He moved out and filed for divorce.

During the nine-month separation, some of Mike's friends encouraged him to proceed with divorce, claiming, "No woman's ever going to do that to me." But alone in his apartment, Mike's mind cleared. "I realized I could be okay without her," he says. "I let go of the power she had over me." From this position of strength, he started to see forgiveness as a decision he could make for himself, regardless of whether they reunited.

He also started thinking about Melissa as a separate person with her own history, her own difficulties, and her own reasons for the affair. Melissa's father was an alcoholic, and her supervisor had apparently become a father figure who gave her some of the love and attention she had yearned for from her dad. "I couldn't hear that at first," says Mike. "But eventually it made some sense."

Now it's been more than five years since Mike forgave Melissa and moved back in. He now believes "it takes more strength to forgive and rebuild the relationship than to say, 'Fuck you, I'm gone.' You're taking such a risk of being hurt. It's a powerful thing to do."

Gandhi would have agreed. "The weak can never forgive," he said. "Forgiveness is the attribute of the strong."

People talk about forgiveness as if it were a discrete event: "Have you forgiven him yet?" A sense of resolution and closure can be reached, but forgiveness is a process, sometimes a lifelong process of reflection and renewal. Often, as in Mike's case, anger comes in waves, returning again and again, so the forgiver must repeatedly cultivate compassion—for the same person, for the same offense. The forgiver must repeatedly open his heart, staying vigilant to make sure it doesn't ease shut when he or she is not watching.

Some people forgive repeatedly and persistently through prayer. Each day they deliberately pray for someone who hurt them, asking for blessings for that person. Some people simply imagine good things happening for that person. I can't explain why these things work, but they seem to: Hoping or praying for good things to happen to someone else gradually opens our own hearts. Eventually, we forget to pray or meditate because there's no more anger in us to serve as a reminder. Then the anger returns, and the prayers return, until the process is complete.

The Seneca Indian José Hobday says of his spiritual tradition, "Every time you remember a wrong, you are asked to forgive it. From my experience, wrongs will return to the mind for years and years and years. Each recall asks for forgiveness . . . until you let it go."[1]

This advice echoes Jesus's answer to Peter when he told him to forgive, not seven times, but "seventy times seven."

Another factor that gets in the way of forgiveness is a lack of justice. Bruce committed statutory rape, which is a felony, instigated numerous instances of indecent exposure, and took sexual liberties with a minor. Yet he never faced a judge, served prison time, or performed community service—largely because, when I was young, he convinced me not to tell anyone. A recent *Time* magazine poll found that 65 percent of the American public favors the death penalty for child sexual abuse. The death penalty! Only murder was considered punishable by death by a larger percentage of people.[2] I certainly did not think Bruce should be put to death, but for a while the fact that "there had been no justice" got in the way of my ability to forgive him. I didn't want to "let him off easy."

Yet I now see that reparations and justice should be considered separately from the question of whether to forgive. Jackie Pflug, the airplane hostage who forgave the Palestinian terrorist who shot her, says, "Just because you forgive somebody doesn't allow them to get off the hook. He still needs to be responsible for his actions."[3]

Even David Berkowitz makes a distinction between forgiveness and justice. Berkowitz is the self-named "Son of Sam" murderer who killed six people in a yearlong rampage that ended with his arrest in August 1977. He recently said from prison that he believes "Christ has chosen" to forgive him. Nevertheless, he added, "I truly deserve punishment and death."[4]

Yet the lack of justice, or reparations, or punishment, often gets in the way of forgiveness. "How can I forgive when he hasn't been punished?" people ask me. One answer: Consider how much you're punishing yourself by not forgiving. By clinging to all that hatred, are you really helping anyone to heal?

On the other hand, sometimes the question of forgiveness clouds the question of justice. I found this to be true in President Clinton's case. When Clinton apologized to his cabinet members for lying to them about his affair with Monica Lewinsky, Vice President Gore's response was paternal. "Mr. President, I think most of America has forgiven you, but you've got to get your act together."[5]

What Gore seemed to be saying was that forgiveness was not the point. I think he was right. Sometimes the request for forgiveness, or ruminations over whether to forgive, mask underlying issues: Is this person trustworthy? Will his behavior change? Shall we continue to work with him? The question of forgiveness can create a smokescreen, obscuring more practical issues of accountability and contractual agreements for the future. Forgiveness is important, to the guilty party or to those who care about him, but justice, reparations, and responsibility are also important.

Politics can also complicate the forgiveness process. Should men—individually or collectively—apologize to women for rape, for battery, for sexual harassment, for a history of legal, educational, and economic discrimination? And should women (or their surviving family members) forgive? Under what conditions? What would happen if men did apologize, and women did forgive? Could forgiveness be a healing tool in the so-called battle of the sexes? The Million Man March and the Promise Keepers have introduced the subject of male atonement for sexist "sins" like adultery and the use of pornography. Some of the Promise Keepers' wives have talked with reporters about forgiving their formerly abusive husbands. But many women greet these public acts of contrition with skepticism. They resent the perceived pressure to forgive, and the implied pressure to tolerate male abuse.

> *Forgive you?—Oh, of course, dear,*
> *A dozen times a week!*
> *We women were created*
> *Forgiveness but to speak.*[6]

That's a poem written by the journalist Ella Higginson about a hundred years ago. Many women still seem to share this sentiment: Forgiveness is a female role, but an unfair one. In *Sex in the Forbidden Zone,* the psychiatrist Peter Rutter says women are expected to "silently absorb the injuries" inflicted by men—and to forgive those men, individually and collectively.[7] In *The Courage to Heal,* considered by some the bible of recovery from childhood sexual abuse, Ellen Bass and Laura Davis seem suspicious of forgiveness, and mistrusting. "Trying to forgive is a futile short-circuit of the healing process," they warn, adding, "the only necessity as far as healing is concerned is forgiving *yourself.*"[8]

Obviously, I don't think forgiveness is a futile short-circuit of the healing process. Sometimes I had trouble conveying my newfound faith in forgiveness to my friends. When I was suffering from the emotional breakdown triggered by seeing Bruce for the first time, my feminist friends were my most supportive allies. Women tend to be good at "troubles talk," as Deborah Tannen calls it. But later, when I forgave Bruce, some of those friends no longer seemed to understand.

I had a hard time understanding it myself. If I forgave Bruce, was I somehow permitting abuse to continue? Was it possible that he was still molesting other girls, and tricking me into believing he was not? If I stopped naming him in public, was I being manipulated into silence? And if in this book I chose not to name him out of respect for his privacy, did this represent another victory on his part?

Are women more forgiving than men? No studies have yet answered that question. Men get credit for forgiving quickly—the stereotype depicts them feuding in the boardroom or on the baseball field, then having a beer together afterward—but women are the ones who seem to work harder at relationships. Raised to value connection, women might feel more driven to seek and find forgiveness because of our conditioning to be peacemakers, healers, nurturers. So far, in my experience, women are the ones who say most readily, "There's someone I need to forgive," or, "I really need to read that book." Maybe men are less likely to make such remarks because they see them as revealing weakness (admitting that they have an emotional need).

Regardless of potential gender differences, the act of forgiveness frees women from the victim stance in relation to men. It empowers us to love, to release old anger, to choose what sort of relationship, if any, we want for the future. From this place of choice and power, women become models of strength for other women. Early feminists were right to say that "the personal is political." Because personal forgiveness frees women, it has political implications for improved relationships between women and men.

In trying to rectify discrimination and injustice, many of the world's greatest leaders—Mahatma Gandhi, Martin Luther King, the Dalai Lama, Nelson Mandela, Desmond Tutu—have demonstrated love, compassion, and forgiveness. They were popular and effective because they combined outspoken resistance to oppression with gentleness. Female leaders—whether on a national, international, or local level—could similarly demonstrate the power of forgiveness.

Yet some of my most ardent feminist friends have remained wary of my newfound enthusiasm for forgiveness. While respectful of me, they have seemed unwilling to perceive Bruce as a flawed and all too human being, worthy of compassion.

"I have no desire to feel sorry for people who commit sex crimes," said one woman.

"I would be more interested in a book called *Revenge*," said another, only half-joking.

One male feminist friend wrote to me, "My heart goes out to you, Mariah. If he has suffered, he brought it on himself, and he dragged others (his family as well as his victims) under in the process. I care about you and hope you get to the other side of this process. I don't care at all about him."

What does this mean, "I don't care at all about him"? What kind of people are we if we care only about the people who treat us well and not about the people who do cruel or thoughtless deeds? If not forgiving, how should we be? Mistrusting? Vengeful? Films like *Thelma and Louise* and *The First Wives' Club* validate women's rage and feed their revenge fantasies. They say, in effect, "We're mad as hell, and we're not going to take it anymore." I find them somewhat cathartic and enjoyable myself. But who would want to live the life of Thelma or Louise: abused, enraged, murderous, then dead? There must be a better way.

I believe we can forgive with open eyes as well as an open heart. I think there's a way to separate the act of forgiveness from rational decisions such as whether to stay married. I think women should forgive men for sexist behaviors and attitudes—not so that men can continue to take advantage of women with impunity, but so that women can take charge of their lives and stop feeling—and being—victimized. I think men need to offer apologies and reparations, and women need to become smart enough, big-hearted enough, and humble enough to forgive. Women can set boundaries, refusing to be abused, but also refusing to close their hearts to people who are filled with anger, hatred, or confusion. As women find compassion for the men who have hurt them, they will also begin to notice—and forgive themselves for—their own anger, hatred, and confusion. This sort of process can go a long way toward ending the battle of the sexes.

Considering the particular tensions between black men and women, the educator Marita Golden writes in *Saving Our Sons,*

> We black women must forgive black men for not protecting us against slavery, racism, white men, our confusion, their doubts. And black men must forgive black women for our own sometimes dubious choices, divided loyalties, and lack of belief in their possibilities. Only when our sons and our daughters know that forgiveness is real, existent,

and that those who love them practice it, can they form bonds as men and women that really can save and change our community.[9]

Forgiveness can be endlessly complicated, since human beings are, but there's just one more complication I want to explore here: the problems that arise when the person asking for forgiveness doesn't stop there. She wants forgiveness, but she also wants something else: reassurance perhaps, or friendship, or permission to forgive herself.

When I was in college, I became good friends with a thirty-year-old I'll call Grace. For more than twelve years, we had an intense and rewarding but also sometimes difficult friendship that ended abruptly when she wrote me an angry letter stating that she wanted no further contact. Not understanding her anger but weary of a pattern of emotional drama, I respected her wishes and let the friendship go.

Over the next ten years, I thought of her on her birthday and at many other times, sometimes wondering whether I should have handled things differently, before or after her abrupt withdrawal. I wondered whether, after having once been so close, we would allow our long and meaningful friendship to end on such a sour note. We had talked often of endings, in part because her brother had died at a young age, and we had shared a desire to keep all relationships as clean and honest as possible. Yet it never seemed right to contact her, so I didn't.

While I was working on this book, Grace wrote to me via my literary agent. In the letter, she apologized for having aborted our relationship and for the things she had written in anger. She said she had many fond memories of me and thanked me for my generosity and wisdom during those years. She said she'd like to hear from me—she enclosed numerous methods by which I could contact her—but added that she could understand if I did not respond. In any case, she said, she wished me well.

It seemed a perfect apology. She had expressed remorse and accepted responsibility without demanding anything, even forgiveness. She offered no excuses. It felt just right.

Relieved and happy, I immediately wrote back via e-mail, accepting her apology. I also offered an apology for my own part in our dispute. I included birthday greetings, calculating that she was about to turn fifty.

Writing my own letter to Grace felt even better than receiving hers. How satisfying to forgive someone who clearly wanted to be forgiven! How big-hearted I felt! How good of me to forgive her, and so quickly! And how magnanimous I felt, for offering my apology to her too!

The wait for her reply seemed long. During those few days, I realized that there had been strings attached to my forgiveness. I wanted her to be pleased and grateful. I was waiting to be thanked for my marvelousness.

Soon she gave me what I wanted: an enthusiastic reception. "I didn't realize how much I was hoping you would reply to my letter," she wrote. "I am very happy and feel that of all the birthday presents I received and loving good wishes for my, yes, fiftieth birthday, yours I treasure most. The gift of forgiveness." She went on to tell me about her marriage, her business, and her home, and said I was welcome to visit anytime.

From there, the relationship faltered. Busy, I didn't respond to her subsequent e-mail messages right away. Wary of becoming entangled in another demanding friendship, I sent brief friendly notes, but I ignored her repeated requests for my phone number. She responded with anger.

"So she has not changed," noted one friend.

I couldn't be sure whether she had changed or not, but I had changed. As a self-employed writer and speaker, I'm very protective of my time. Over the years, I've grown conscious of my right to say no—whether that means not giving out my phone number, not responding to e-mail right away, or not resuming old friendships. But like many women, and like many people who have been sexually abused, I have trouble setting boundaries in a way that's both firm and kind. Sometimes I'm harsher than I need to be, saying *No!* instead of just "No." Sometimes I say yes, then feel resentful. Sometimes I say no, then feel guilty. I can also feel angry about people's requests, instead of simply declining them. So it's entirely possible that I didn't handle the situation with Grace very well.

Now that some time has passed, I can see that just as I had not granted my forgiveness without hoping for something in return, Grace had attached strings to her apology as well. She didn't just want to resolve things between us, she wanted to resume a friendship. Apparently, my forgiveness had meant to Grace, "Let's take up where we left off."

My forgiveness was sincere, as was my apology, but I was afraid to reenter a potentially difficult relationship. The experience taught me to see a pattern that I came to think of as "Please forgive me and. . . ." In this case, it was: "Please forgive me and make yourself available to be friends again. Please forgive me and listen to my stories about the past ten years. Please forgive me and answer my e-mails right away, and give me your address and phone number." In addition to forgiveness, Grace seemed to want support, attention, time, and friendship. She wasn't wrong to want those things; I just didn't want the same things, at least not right away.

Other people ask for other things. A spouse might say, "Please forgive me and trust me again." An ex-spouse might say, "Please forgive me and let me share custody of our children." A parent or grandparent might say, "Please forgive me and take care of me now that I'm old." In fact, the people who say, "Please forgive me. Period." may be in the minority.

Bruce was also someone who said, "Please forgive me and. . . ." After I forgave him, he asked for a friendship with me. I was never sure why. Maybe because of the intense experience we had shared and the affectionate feelings it had produced in both of us. Maybe because he discovered in our conversations that we had much in common. Maybe he was trying to offer the friendship we might have had if he had been a trustworthy mentor and we had stayed friends throughout our lives. But I also wondered whether he wanted me to stay in his life to demonstrate that I was forgiving him over and over again. I wondered whether he wanted to make sure I stayed close enough, and attached enough, that I'd never act vengeful again.

With Grace, I initially chose what could be called a middle path: responding in a friendly way but infrequently, and ignoring her requests for more contact. I'm usually much more direct. But after carefully drafting several e-mails in which I explained that I forgave her but didn't want to resume the friendship, I deleted them all. No matter how hard I tried to be kind, that message sounded cruel, like a rebuff, something that could trigger more hurt, and another ugly ending. Instead, I tried to send this meta-message: "I'm delighted you wrote, I've forgiven you, I care about you, and I've moved on."

It was important to me neither to go away mad, as she had done, nor to hurt her feelings, if possible. I found myself forgiving her again—for being presumptuous and aggressive about her desired reconciliation with me, and for wanting more than forgiveness. I reminded myself not to take it personally: That's just who she is (or how she is with me, or how I perceive her). At the same time, I needed to establish my own boundaries: to keep the doors of my heart open, but to make wise decisions about how and with whom I spent my time.

The following year, after about ten months of no contact, she sent me a pleasant e-mail greeting on my own birthday. It might have symbolized another question or request; I wasn't sure. But I chose to interpret it as an indication that she remained openhearted too. Or maybe my nonresponsiveness had indeed hurt her feelings again and her greeting indicated that she had forgiven me for *that*. In any case, I responded with another friendly note and began to open to the possibility of a friendship, if that were to reemerge. After that, we exchanged a few more tentative e-mails, and finally I gave her my phone number. I don't know where, if anywhere, the relationship is going now, but the forgiveness on both sides feels genuine, and I'm grateful for that.

Responding to Bruce's "please forgive me and . . ." request was more difficult.

Chapter 11

RECONCILIATION OR GOOD-BYE?

*I*f my story were a Hollywood movie, Bruce and I would kiss, make up, then make love. That's the fairy tale version of forgiveness. It includes a dramatic, romantic reconciliation: blissful, happily-ever-after.

In real life, romance was out of the question. Friendship, however, seemed within the realm of possibility. As we felt ourselves moving toward forgiveness, Bruce proposed that we stay in touch, remaining "friends." I pondered the offer. In many ways, it appealed to me. I had benefited from our contact. Our letters and phone calls, though emotionally difficult, were ultimately so healing and gratifying that I was reluctant to let him go. Like Bruce, I wanted to sustain some sort of relationship, but it was hard to imagine what form that could take.

By this point, after more than six months of talking with him, I was feeling a deep, unexpected sense of gratitude to the man who had molested me for three years, then later helped me heal from that abuse. Some psychologists might diagnose this as the Stockholm Syndrome—the phenomenon of developing an emotional attachment to your captor—but the way I saw it, Bruce had ultimately become a different sort of teacher and mentor for me. By participating in my healing process, he gave me what I had wanted when I was young: compassion, wisdom, and companionship. He did all the things I'd wanted him to do then: listened, cared about my feelings, told me the truth, respected my boundaries. Plus he gave me the enormous gift of assistance with my healing.

As I was wondering what, if any, future Bruce and I had together, Sheldon Kennedy, a professional hockey player from Canada, came forward with revelations about having been abused by his coach. For twelve years, beginning when Kennedy was fourteen, Graham James had molested him. Clearly, Kennedy was deeply wounded and enraged. Everywhere I went, I saw Kennedy on television, talking about the devastating consequences of childhood sexual abuse. I even appeared with him on *Dateline,* offering expert testimony on widespread coach-athlete abuse. It gave me a chance to practice what I'm now preaching: outspoken resistance to abuse combined with compassion and forgiveness.

Graham James was convicted and sent to prison. In an interview with the *Washington Post,* he said he'd still like to be friends with Kennedy. "As ridiculous and impossible as that sounds, that's how I feel," said James. "I always hope that someday something can be done to bring about a reconciliation."

James's proposal did sound ridiculous and impossible. It made me wonder: *Was it similarly ridiculous and impossible for me even to consider an ongoing friendship with Bruce?*

I said to my friend Nancy Kass, "I like Bruce. I think it would have been nice to be friends with him, if he hadn't molested me."

She laughed gently. "Yeah, Mariah, but that's a big 'if.'"

A famous photo shows a nine-year-old Vietnamese girl running, naked and crying, from an American-led assault on her village. Her clothes have been burned off by napalm. Her arms flap wildly at her sides. Her mouth is a huge hole, screaming. The Associated Press photographer Nick Ut later won a Pulitzer Prize for this work.

John Plummer, the Air Force colonel who ordered the napalm bombing of the village, had been a twenty-four-year-old helicopter pilot during the war. His primary job was to order allied bombing strikes. Like everyone else, he saw the photo in newspapers—and then in numerous exhibits and collections. Over the years, the photo haunted him, giving him nightmares and, he says, triggering excessive drinking as he engaged in a futile effort to forget the many people who had been hurt in the bombings he had ordered.

Years later, in a 1996 television broadcast, Plummer learned that the nine-year-old girl, Pham Thi Kim Phuc, survived the war, grew up, and moved to Toronto. He saw the thick white scars on her neck. He learned that she had endured seventeen operations on her skin, and that she lives with pain. "Of course, I was so glad she was alive," he recalls. "But I knew right then that I was going to have to find her."[1]

A week before Veterans' Day, Plummer learned that Kim planned to appear at the Vietnam Memorial in Washington, D.C., ninety minutes from his home in Purcellville, Virginia. Plummer was standing in the crowd, along with his wife and some veteran friends, when she took the stage. She had no idea he was in the audience. But she told the crowd, "If I could talk face-to-face with the pilot who dropped the bombs, I would tell him we cannot change history, but we should try to do good things for the present and the future to promote peace."

Plummer scribbled a note to her and passed it forward. "Kim, I am that man," the note said.

After the speech, she read the note as she was being escorted away. "I couldn't move anymore," she recalls. "I stop and I turn, and he looked at me."

The former soldier, now forty-nine, and the former child, now thirty-three, embraced. "She just opened her arms to me. I fell into her arms sobbing," said Plummer. "All I could say was, 'I'm so sorry. I'm just so sorry.'"

She patted his back and told him, "It's all right. I forgive, I forgive."

That day they talked and prayed for two hours. In the subsequent year, they stayed in touch and "became friends," according to newspaper reports. This impressive story feeds into a popular belief: If you really forgive, then of course you would want an ongoing relationship with the person who hurt you. And the two of you could become friends. And live happily ever after.

But forgiveness and reconciliation do not necessarily go hand in hand. They are not synonymous. To forgive is to welcome someone back into your heart. To reconcile is to reestablish a close relationship with that person. Often, when one person has permanently injured another, the relationship cannot be repaired. Feelings of affection, if they ever existed, are long gone. Trust cannot be reestablished. Or the victim simply needs space and time to heal. In those cases, while forgiveness remains desirable and possible, reconciliation does not. This is one of the many beauties of forgiveness: The forgiver becomes free to decide for herself whether to reestablish a close relationship. No longer trapped by the past but also not trapped by others' ideas of how the future should unfold, she is free to assess for herself the prospects for a good, healthy relationship.

In other words, we can forgive and still say good-bye. We can forgive and still protect ourselves from further abuse.

Nevertheless, reconciliation can be appealing. Reconciliation can remind the forgiver how generous or openhearted her forgiveness was, and it can remind the forgiven one that they were forgiven. It can give both parties a sense of restoration, normalcy, things returning to their previous state.

We hear incredible stories of reconciliations. We marvel at the victims: If someone dropped a bomb on *us*, could *we* forgive them later? We breathe a sigh of relief with the perpetrator: How wonderful it must feel to be forgiven for the many bombs we've dropped on other people.

Cardinal Joseph Bernardin offers an amazing and heartwarming story in his book *The Gift of Peace.* Steven Cook accused Bernardin of sexual misconduct in November 1993. Cook claimed to have been led to Bernardin's bedroom in 1975, when he was a college student, and forced to submit to a sex act. His accusation, which he later recanted and acknowledged to be false, was broadcast worldwide, leading millions of people to hear Bernardin's name for the first time in connection with the allegation.

When Bernardin learned of the accusation, he prayed, reviewing the biblical promise that "the truth will set you free." He then sent out a press release saying, "While I have not seen the suit and do not know the details of the allegation, there is one thing I do know, and I state categorically: I have never abused anyone in all my life, anywhere, any time, any place."[2]

The following day, Bernardin intuited that his young accuser might somehow be "a pawn in this terrible game. If I was right, he needed prayers as much as I did right then. I felt a genuine impulse to pray with and comfort him." Bernardin wrote Cook a letter to that effect; later he would learn that Cook's lawyer never passed it along. The letter had read, in part: "As I thought it over, I began to think that you must be suffering a great deal. The idea came to me yesterday that it would be a good thing if I visited you personally. The purpose of the visit would be strictly pastoral—to show my concern for you and to pray with you. If you are interested in such a visit, please let me know. I will come to you if you wish."[3]

What an incredible response! How many of us would, under those circumstances, understand the pain of our accuser and offer to go pray with him? Bernardin sounds as saintly as Linda Biehl, who prayed, "Father, forgive them, they know not what they've done," when she learned that her daughter had been murdered. Bernardin's lawyers, by contrast, had proposed a "scorched earth" strategy in which they would attack Cook's history and character. In another incredible show of wisdom, Bernardin, determined not to "deter persons who had really been abused from coming forward," declined that option.[4]

The case unraveled owing to lack of evidence, and Cook dropped the charges. As it turned out, Cook had in fact been sexually abused by a young priest during seminary school, had left the church, and had pressed charges against that priest. But according to Bernardin, Cook was advised by some of Bernardin's political opponents to include him in the case to garner more attention.

When Bernardin and Cook finally met, after the charges had been dropped, Cook was sick with AIDS. He had had a "difficult life," says Bernardin, and was "a lost sheep." Bernardin began the meeting by saying he harbored no ill feelings toward Cook. Cook apologized and explained his history—which included a hypnotist who had led him to "remember" being abused by Bernardin. He admitted that he knew Bernardin had never abused him, and he apologized again. Bernardin gave him a Bible. They said mass together.

Over the next few months, the two kept in touch. When Bernardin received his diagnosis of pancreatic cancer, Cook's "was one of the first letters I received. He had only a few months to live when he wrote it, filled with sympathy and encouragement for me." When Cook died of

AIDS, he was reconciled with the church as well as with Bernardin. Within another year, Bernardin was dead too. In his memoirs, written in the last months of his life, he said of his experience with Cook: "Never in my entire priesthood have I witnessed a more profound reconciliation."

Most of us are neither priests nor priestly. And our own challenges may be more difficult to deal with than Bernardin's. Sometimes personal injuries, inflicted by people who know us, are even more devastating than public injuries by strangers. In fact, our most enduring wounds usually come from people who know us—people who are able to gain enough trust and access to wound us most deeply.

When we do reconcile with these people, it can be a long, difficult process. Mike, who forgave his wife for having an affair with her supervisor, now describes their marriage as "stronger than it was." He now sees the marriage "more realistically," however, and "would not say that it's perfect." He has also gained some detachment. "She had the affair for her own reasons. I had some involvement, but it wasn't really about me. I no longer take it personally."

Now living with Melissa again, Mike has learned to grant her freedom without constantly questioning her about her whereabouts. When asked whether Melissa is "on probation," Mike laughs. "Clearly there's a possibility that something could happen again, and I do have a little ounce of worry about that, but if she were on probation, that would mean I hadn't really forgiven her. And I have. I've stopped blaming her. I've stopped thinking about it. I've stopped using it against her."

As people forgive, they regain their sense of self-respect and power. "I realized I could be okay without her," Mike said. "I let go of the power she had over me." From this position of strength, he decided to forgive. Whether to reconcile became a separate decision, one that he and his wife negotiated based on their individual and mutual needs, and the needs of the children.

One of Mike's needs was to reestablish a boundary: no affairs. He knows that Melissa might violate that boundary again. If she does, "I wouldn't necessarily say that the marriage would be over, though I'm surprised to be saying that," responds Mike. "We'd just have to see." But if she were to violate the boundary repeatedly, their hope for a mutually respectful relationship would eventually die. Unlike forgiveness, which depends only on one person opening his or her heart, reconciliation usually depends on forgiveness plus boundaries.

Often the original transgression involves a boundary violation: One person's personal space or home or wallet or psyche or sense of trust is somehow encroached upon by another person. If trust is going to be renewed, and if a close relationship is going to be reestablished, the one who was hurt usually has to say to the other, one way or another, "I will not allow you to exploit me again."

If reconciliation is not an option—if one person is dead, or uninterested in having further contact—then boundary-setting becomes irrelevant. Forgiveness can proceed freely, without conditions. But if a victim and wrongdoer hope to heal a relationship, they must clarify how they will treat each other in the future.

The victim will not always succeed in setting effective boundaries. The wrongdoer may try to take advantage of that person's kindness, or may not know how to act respectful, or may simply make mistakes. The victim may choose to forgive again anyway. But at least he has exhibited enough self-respect to say, "This is how I want to be treated."

Eleanor eventually set numerous boundaries in her marriage to the jazz musician. "If we had an argument, I tried to work it out that day, thanks to the twelve-step program, plus childhood habits of not going to bed angry. But when an addict becomes violent, you're preoccupied with safety and survival for your kids and yourself. Forgiveness doesn't easily come into your heart."

To the extent that she succeeded in forgiving her husband, she says, it was because she realized that alcoholism is a disease, and because she was able to set boundaries. She didn't choose the ultimate boundary—divorce—but instead got a legal protective order when he relapsed after many years of sobriety. It stated that he could ingest no alcohol or drugs in their home, nor could he arrive home under the influence of drugs or alcohol, nor could he abuse or harass anyone. "Just because you forgive doesn't mean you don't take action to protect yourself," Eleanor explains.

Few friends understood Eleanor's attitude toward her husband. "I know there are those who disparaged and even ridiculed me because I did forgive him," she says. "People were uncomprehending that I wasn't vengeful. They thought it was a character flaw, that I should have left him, or hit him back, or punished him. In fact, I tried all of those things, but they did not solve the problem."

Along with protecting herself physically, she did her best to protect herself emotionally. "Abusers are very good at convincing you that if only you were different, they wouldn't drink or abuse drugs," she says. "But I knew better. I had a normal, happy, and healthy childhood. I knew that no excuse could justify his behavior when he was drinking. Just because I might be five minutes late didn't give him an excuse to be abusive. I had to give myself permission to be human. And as a woman and someone who was eager to please, I had to learn to insist that he respect me."

Eleanor tried to satisfy her own needs for physical and emotional security while also loving her husband—"a gentle, sweet, nonviolent man when he was sober." She came to understand that alcoholism should not be taken personally. "In my mind, I dealt with it as if he had a brain tumor. If he had had a brain tumor, and if he had been out of control and threatening to abuse us, then calling the police—along with seeking treatment—would be the appropriate, sensible thing to do."

During my contact with Bruce, I established several boundaries: rules about how and when we would have contact. In general, I didn't want him to call me, only to write to me. Our phone conversations were intense, and I didn't want to worry, neither in the midst of my busy workdays nor during relaxed evenings at home, that any caller might be Bruce. I preferred receiving letters that I could read and ponder when I was ready. During one three-week period, I asked him not to contact me at all since I was finishing *Embracing Victory* and didn't want to be distracted by emotional trauma. I set similar (though less strict) boundaries with friends and family; I simply become reclusive when I'm a few weeks away from a book deadline.

Bruce's rules for me were different. He welcomed phone calls, and as it turns out, I called him many times. I actually enjoyed talking to him on the phone, even though it was stressful. I just needed to establish boundaries about it so that he would not invade my psychic space, as he had done when I was young.

The fact that he respected my boundaries surprised me. One time, when I called him after turning in the manuscript, I thanked him for not having contacted me during the weeks leading up to the deadline.

"Of course," he said. "You asked me not to."

"I appreciate that you're respecting my boundaries," I explained.

"This is just who I am," he replied, somewhat perplexed. "If you tell me not to call, I won't call."

He had changed, apparently, as had I.

Still, forgiveness and boundaries are not sufficient for reconciliation. Many people in Mike's position, or in Eleanor's position, leave their spouse. Some say "I forgive you" first, then leave. Some just leave. The decision to reconcile, like the decision to forgive, is a personal one.

In my case, it wasn't until after our therapy session that the answer to my question about whether to reconcile became clear. It wasn't until after therapy that I fully forgave Bruce, and somehow forgiveness had to come first, before I could decide about reconciliation. For Eleanor, forgiveness and reconciliation were daily, ongoing, overlapping challenges, but I suspect that for most of us the question of reconciliation can't really be answered until we have forgiven.

On the day of our therapy session, I was a wreck. By the time I arrived at Margaret's office at a little before nine in the morning, I had already been up for seven hours, anxious and upset. Bruce was waiting for me on the sidewalk. After I parked the car, we looked at each other across the parking lot, as we had done a couple of months before. His eyes were friendly, familiar, anxious, apologetic, eager. Mine were red.

As I got closer, Bruce opened his arms toward me in greeting. I shook my head. "I don't want to hug you this time," I said, reminding him. "It was too hard last time."

He nodded. It felt good to do that, to tell him not to touch me— something I had lacked the skills, power, and courage to do as a child. It felt good to do so kindly, without anger. No more hugs, no more scent memories, no more head on my shoulder, no more hand on my arm. A clear boundary set by me, respected by him. A new way of being together.

Inside, I introduced Bruce to Margaret, and she set more boundaries: We were there to help me resolve my feelings about the abuse. I appreciated that, because I was afraid Bruce would try to frame the issue as "our problem." I was well aware that he had suffered from remorse, shame, and the negative reactions of his colleagues and family. But Margaret reminded us that this session was for me.

At my request, we began with prayers. First we shared a long meditative silence, during which I sobbed. Then Bruce said a prayer aloud, asking for God's help with our process. I liked his sincerity and humility. It helped me trust him, hearing how he prayed.

In planning the session beforehand, I had heard about two models for such confrontations. The first includes two elements: acknowledgment (the victim says, "This is what you did") and apology (the perpetrator says, "I'm sorry"). The second model includes three elements, all from the victim: acknowledgment ("this is what you did"), consequences ("these were the results"), and update ("this is how I feel about it now").

I decided to combine these two approaches. I wanted to talk about the abuse and its effects on me, and I wanted to hear an apology. By now, Bruce had apologized several times, in letters, in phone calls, and in our other face-to-face meeting, at his office, so my need for another apology was not great, but it seemed like a good idea to hear him apologize one final time, without the confusion of his touching me at the same time, and with Margaret as a witness. I also wanted to offer Bruce some time to talk about his experience, in case his explanation could help me understand what had happened—though I was ambivalent about this, fearing that anything he said would sound like hollow rationalization. As it turned out, Margaret also had an agenda: to obtain from Bruce a specific confession.

Mostly, I talked. During one long "this is what happened and these were the results" speech, I recounted the many times he molested me and betrayed my trust. I talked and cried for a half-hour straight. Throughout, Bruce listened intently, leaning forward in his chair, his eyes on me. He never interrupted. The only time his body language changed was when I talked about how agonizing it had been for me to baby-sit for his kids. He used to drive me home afterward, then molest me in the car. Being in his house, caring for his children, chatting with his wife, then getting molested by him on the way home—all of this had been particularly guilt-inducing and painful for me. As I talked about that, Bruce looked down at his hands, as if again in prayer.

When it was his turn to talk, Bruce said he had felt "in over his head" in his coaching job, inadequate and incompetent. He said that he had enjoyed my company tremendously and had perceived the sex as "a gift" to me. He reminisced about good times, smiling and laughing. Nervous, he rambled, talking about many things, some of which were utterly irrelevant to the subject at hand.

I began to feel disoriented and withdrawn. Margaret's presence was essential. She interrupted and insisted that he name exactly what he had done to me, in criminal terms. "Do you admit that you engaged in statutory rape?" she said. "That you committed a felony?" Trembling, and through clenched teeth, he said yes.

He also apologized to me, and asked how he could help me heal.

"You're doing it," I replied. "This is helping."

The session wasn't perfect, but it was cathartic. I didn't say "I forgive you," but the session carried me in that direction. I felt the way the cyclist Maureen Vergara did when she was thinking about forgiving the driver who ran into her. I became ready to forgive Bruce no matter what—even if the story didn't add up perfectly, even if I couldn't categorize and explain everything in one neat package, even if he was still hiding things and not facing things, not doing everything exactly according to my preferences.

At the end of the two hours, we thanked each other for the courage it had taken to participate. We left unresolved the issue of what, if anything, to do next. At his request, we shook hands. The handshake felt strangely businesslike, but I was willing to touch him that much—to extend myself, literally, in his direction.

As I drove home, I heard "To Sir, with Love" on the radio. The song tells the story of a girl who has a crush on her teacher. He responds with kindness, but professionally. It used to make me cry every time I heard it. This time, I just appreciated its beautiful tune and laughed at the irony of hearing it right then.

When I reached my house, instead of going back to work, I went to bed and slept for two hours. When I woke up, I realized that my process of forgiving Bruce was complete, or nearly so. I felt lighter, happier, at peace—and physically exhausted, as if my anger, resentment, and bitterness had been washed off my body in a torrential rain. Or as if I had been clinging to a rope, getting rope-burn on my hands, tensing the muscles in my arms and shoulders, clinging, clinging—then let go. I gave up all that tension, all that resentment, all that attachment to the events of many years ago. What a relief.

My forgiveness included not only the past but also Bruce's current imperfections. Even in the therapy session, he had said things that made me think, *He still doesn't completely get it.* But as my heart opened, I found myself forgiving him for that, and more: for not being the model recovering sex offender, for not being willing to become a spokesperson on the issue of sexual abuse, for wanting me not to keep naming him in public, for acting needy and wounded, for clinging to my arm in his office. It became obvious to me that he had his own limitations, as do I. As I forgave him for the past, it became relatively easy to forgive him for the present as well.

Later that night I called Bruce, suddenly worried about his potential for suicide. I hadn't said anything cruel or surprising in the session, but I needed to see if he was okay. Or maybe I just needed to reconnect with the person with whom I'd spent an incredibly intense morning. Bruce was grateful for the call, and for the session. He compared it to bloodletting: a painful but necessary process to rid the body of toxins. He also told me that when I had been crying, he had wanted to comfort me by holding me, but knew that I wouldn't have wanted that. I told him about having had that fantasy myself—about wanting him to cradle me, to soothe my pain that way, but knowing it was not right. So I received his statement like a verbal hug. Somehow it was just what I needed.

Soon after our therapy session, I received this thank-you note from Bruce:

Dear Mariah,

The emotion of the day was incredible, but the caring phone call, the smile when leaving, and the shared words of hope and concern carried me home.

I hope you know without question that I take *full* responsibility for the acts and for the pain and sadness that I have caused you. You do not have to spend any time working on forgiving yourself. You were not at fault.

I will continue to pray that your days are peaceful, full of hope, and that those around you will share in your smiles, sense of humor, love, and caring.

Perhaps someday we will be able to share parts of our lives as we grow older. But I recognize, accept, and respect that this will or will not happen at your choice. It is very important to me that your life is free of all the negative emotions you have had to deal with in the past.

Mariah, my sincere thanks again. Know that I will always regret hurting you and that I will carry you in my prayers.

Take good care of yourself,

With care,

Bruce

Again, I was touched by this letter. In particular, I appreciated his sensitivity about any future relationship we might have, his recognition that that had to be my decision too. But now what? Should we be friends or not?

My friend Constantine Kyropoulos, a psychiatrist, predicted that being friends would put me in the position of having to forgive Bruce repeatedly. Or that, alternatively, Bruce could become a convenient target for any of my anger.

I didn't feel angry anymore, but I could foresee that if we had ongoing contact, the emotional dynamics would be tricky. I might indeed feel like I had to forgive him repeatedly. I might feel wounded or betrayed or sad all over again. Or I might get drawn into a nurturing role, taking care of him and his emotional pain. None of this appealed to me.

Nor did more secrecy. Keeping our original secret had been extremely destructive to me. Ever since, I've been committed to openness, directness, honesty. Because Bruce was unwilling to come forward as a child molester, I was afraid I'd end up in the position of hiding our past yet again. I was unwilling to court the possibility that someday I could call his house and be unsure of who would answer the phone and unclear as to how to identify myself. I was unwilling to meet his friends or colleagues or potential future spouse and be introduced as "an old friend," as he had done when I visited him at his office. I needed to say no to secrets and shame. His unwillingness to be more open about his history became an impasse, an irreconcilable difference.

Also, I simply needed to let go of the past. Although I was conflicted about the decision, I knew deep down that I'd feel better, clearer, and ultimately happier and healthier if I ended the relationship. Any emotional work I had left to do would not need to involve him. And because Bruce and I are not relatives and do not live in the same state, I had the advantage of not expecting to run into him; I therefore didn't need to push myself to create some kind of comfortable ongoing relationship with him.

Margaret concurred. She's not the kind of therapist to offer her opinion very often; mostly she followed my lead. Even on the subject of forgiveness, in which I was developing an intellectual interest, she did not engage with me about its use as a healing or therapeutic tool. Instead, she listened when I stated what I wanted, how I felt, and what I thought, and respectfully helped me sort it all out. Yet after meeting Bruce, she did spontaneously offer an opinion that surprised me: While acknowledging that he seemed both sincere and wounded, she said her impression was that he was self-centered and still had bad boundaries.

I saw him through a different lens. Whose view was right? Or were we both right? Was Bruce a kind, caring, remorseful, selfish person who still had bad boundaries? There was no way to know for sure. I was grateful to Margaret for offering that opinion—in part because it showed me how useful it had been for her *not* to offer an opinion during most of my therapy process. Ultimately, her opinion of Bruce was irrelevant. This was my journey, and my decision, regardless of how anyone else perceived Bruce. I needed to forgive for my own sake, no matter what. I also knew that, as Bruce noted, the reconciliation decision was mine alone.

All that was left to do was say good-bye. I wrote Bruce a letter, finally offering him the words, "I forgive you." I explained that, for several reasons, I was reluctant to let go of our contact altogether. We had discovered that we still shared some interests and values. We had been moved by the intense experience of talking and writing to each other. The prospect of developing a respectful adult relationship was, in some ways, appealing. Perhaps, if things had been different, we would have been friends. Yet, I wrote,

> as I weigh the two alternatives—some sort of contact versus no
> contact—I believe that no contact will be better for me, and will

better facilitate the healing I've got left to do. Sometimes healing requires closure, and closure can have a way of opening up other experiences and other wisdom, as yet unimaginable.

You've said that there are many kinds of friendship. Maybe we could think of ourselves as friends of the heart: people who choose, respectfully and with care, not to be in touch except through prayers and kind thoughts.

Then I couldn't send the letter. Was it right to say good-bye, forever, in a letter? What if he never received it? Should I send it FedEx, then track it? I had never said "I forgive you" to him out loud. Wouldn't it be kinder, more complete, if I offered that to him on the phone, rather than in writing?

So I called him.

"I forgive you," I said.

It was about two weeks after our therapy session. I still hadn't mailed my letter. For a moment, he was silent. Finally, he said quietly, "You have no idea how much that means to me."

I nodded, unable to speak.

"I feel so relieved and grateful," he said, adding immediately, "and I do hope it helps you too. I hope you feel some relief now too."

"I do."

"I know that there are many stages of healing, and that you might have more pain about this," said Bruce.

"If I get angry again, I'll forgive you again," I promised. That idea— "forgive again and again"—was from the forgiveness therapy book he had given me early in our forgiveness process.[5] I had been dubious then, and cynical: Was it his place to urge me to forgive him and to send me how-to books on the subject? But I read it anyway—about five times.

I thanked him for having participated in this process with me and said I appreciated the way we talked to each other—with dignity and respect. I told him that the process transformed how I think about him and how I feel about him, and also how I think about the past and how I feel about myself. I told him that I've learned many things that I might not have learned otherwise or that might have taken me much longer to learn, and that I would always be grateful to him for that. I wished him well with his own process of self-forgiveness. "You're a good person," I said. "I wasn't wrong to love you."

Then I added, "I need to tell you that I don't want any further contact with you." Then I started crying, really sobbing. In between sobs, I said, "It's hard to say good-bye. It's weird—in a way you've given me everything I wanted all those years ago: caring, listening, sensitivity to my needs. But I just need to close this door now. I'm closing it gently, not in anger."

"I understand that," he said. "I know that there are consequences to what I did to you, and you're telling me that one of those consequences is that I don't get to be your friend. I can see why. We might be sitting around just chatting someday, and something might trigger painful memories for you. I understand why you don't want to go through that."

He added that if I changed my mind, I would be welcome to contact him. "If you ever want to talk, if you're feeling sad, or if you're having a good day, or if you're in town and just want to spontaneously come by, that's always okay."

I told him not to expect that and repeated that I did forgive him.

"It means so much to me that you say that. I'm so sorry for everything."

"I know," I said. "I accept your apology."

"You'll be in my prayers," he promised.

"Grief is desire," says my friend Richard Hoffman in his beautiful memoir *Half the House*.[6] Until I read that phrase, my own desire confused me. Now I think I understand what Richard means: My desire for Bruce—to have him hold me or soothe my pain or just be available to talk—was a part of my grieving process. As I said good-bye, I was grieving, I now realize, for what had been lost—the generous, humorous teacher who suddenly disappeared from my life, the "lover" who broke my heart, the longtime mentor he might have been—and what I was losing now—this intense, caring adult relationship we had created in the past year. I think I was also grieving some lost pieces of my girlhood, some ineffable innocence.

For a long time, I missed Bruce, and when I missed him, I think I missed primarily the clean adult friendship that never really was. I once attended one of Elisabeth Kubler-Ross's retreats, and she told me, in another context, that the most difficult grieving is for something you never had.

For almost a year, my grieving continued. It took the form of dreaming about Bruce, looking for Bruce in airports, revisiting my decision not to contact him, remembering that he had said I always could. Sometimes I wanted to send him books, such as *Return of the Prodigal Son* and *Mr. Ives' Christmas,* which have meaningful and beautiful forgiveness themes. Sometimes I wanted to reassure him that I was okay, or reassure myself that he was. Sometimes not calling him was a one-day-at-a-time sort of thing, like an addiction I had to get over. Sometimes it felt deeply sad, like euthanasia. I'd killed a relationship that needed to die, but it was still terribly sad.

Yet silence is special, and even sacred. I enjoyed the discipline of the silence, the strength of it, the privacy of it. I still didn't want him calling me and took comfort in the fact that I did now trust him to respect my boundaries. Nor did I want to call him and interrupt his silence, whatever it might contain, or his privacy.

We had done our work, and now we were finished. I felt a deep sense of peace about that, and freedom, which I grew to cherish.

Chapter 12

FREEDOM

The first time I thought about forgiving Bruce was when he asked me to forgive him. I didn't know then how forgiveness would feel. Like the woman who had told me, in answer to my question about her parents' deaths, "I'm okay with it now," that became my goal: to be "okay with" what had happened to me as a teenager. I wanted to accept it, to finish grieving and suffering and raging.

Through forgiveness, I achieved that goal. I'm okay with it now.

But sometimes, when you begin a journey, you can't set your sights on the end because you can't see that far yet. In the process of forgiving Bruce, I realized that forgiveness can lead to a place beyond "okay."

That place is freedom. Once my heart opened, I became free: from the past, from the people who hurt me in the past, from my own tired old grievances. To my surprise, my experience with Bruce affected every one of my relationships, and nearly every encounter I had. I became free to love more and to receive more love. I now find myself giving friends, family members, and strangers room to make mistakes. Whether or not I receive acknowledgment or apology from the other person, I often forgive people for saying the wrong thing, for not saying enough, for

acting rude, for having values different from mine, for soliciting dona-
tions at dinnertime. As I've become better able to accept people as they
are, with compassion and without resentment, I can feel closer to them.
Forgiving Bruce was like turning on a faucet and allowing compassion
to flow in all directions. It cleansed my spirit and changed my view of
the world.

It changed how I do and do not define myself. When I realized that I had
been a victim of sexual abuse, I stopped thinking of myself as an adulteress. Then I learned that some victims were now calling themselves survivors. "I survived" sounds more positive, and more like an achievement,
than "I was victimized."

But now that I have forgiven Bruce, neither "victim" nor "survivor" fits
for me. True, I was victimized, and true, I survived. But I don't feel like a
victim, because the forgiving process empowered me. I don't feel like
a survivor, because I no longer identify with that particular era of my history. Sexual abuse is just one of many things that has happened to me in
my life thus far; it doesn't define me.

For a while, I searched for a third word, beyond *victim* and *survivor.*
What about *forgiver?* Maybe the progression goes from victim to survivor
to forgiver. Yet even that word seems too tied to the past. It's true that I'm
a forgiver. But here's what best describes me now: I'm free.

Freedom is what Peter Biehl was talking about when he said, in regard
to the feelings he and his wife Linda have about the men who murdered
their daughter Amy, "We feel absolutely, completely liberated. We harbor
no grudge, no desire for reparations. We're free. We sleep very well at
night."

Maureen Kaila Vergara discovered the connection between forgiveness and freedom as she began to forgive the driver who ran into her
when she was in training on her bicycle. "The forgiving empowers me
and frees me from this dark negative place," she says. "I am forgiving a
person I thought I would resent for the rest of my life. It's much more
than his saying, 'I'm sorry,' and my replying, 'It's okay.' I feel free. I feel a
calm, inner peace."

If they're lucky, forgivers free themselves from the tendency to get
their feelings hurt easily or habitually to feel like a victim or martyr. They

become less critical of others. Often this seems to happen naturally. The experience of forgiving Mosqueda "has taught me to be more understanding and respectful of other people," says Vergara. "Maybe to slow down and not be as judgmental, give people more of a chance. I find myself trying to make a better effort to forgive on smaller levels with other people in my life."

Forgivers can also transform their relationship with themselves. They allow themselves the daily gaffes (and colossal failures) for which they might have been harshly self-critical in the past. They apologize more readily, and with less shame, because they forgive themselves more readily. They're less defensive about their mistakes and faults. They laugh at themselves more easily. They become free from the prison of perfectionism.

And forgivers free the people around them. I'm thinking of a friend who always seems to see the best in other people. She rarely speaks of others in a negative way, and even when she does, that assessment is immersed in compassion. Being around her, I feel free. I can let go of all my fears of saying or doing something wrong, something stupid, something graceless or inappropriate. I don't worry about hurting her feelings. I can relax, because I sense that she'll forgive me for any mistakes. I feel forgiven in advance. It's a wonderful feeling.

In speaking about awareness in chapter 4, I said that it's important to affix blame. When an interpersonal transgression has occurred, it's important to decide who was responsible for what. Until you know whom you blame, you can't forgive.

I still think this is true. But after I forgave Bruce, I noticed another option. You can also "go directly to compassion," as Cheri Huber puts it, without blaming anyone in the first place. In this case, forgiveness is not necessary. I've come to think of this as the no-blame path to freedom.

For example, a month before I finished writing this book, a drunk driver hit my car from behind, hard, then did a U-turn and fled. I did a U-turn too and chased him, honking my horn. He didn't stop, but I got his license plate number, and ultimately he was charged with felony hit-and-run. He spent one night in jail, and I spent a lot of time getting my car fixed, seeing doctors, nursing my minor injuries, dealing with insurance companies, and ultimately testifying against him in criminal court.

When asked by the police the night of the accident if I wanted to press charges, my answer was immediate. "Of course." He had one previous drunk-driving conviction, and I'll take whatever steps I can to get a drunk driver off the road. But I never blamed the driver, so I never needed to forgive him. I felt enraged when, after hitting me, he fled. But my anger did not harden into the kind of bitterness that requires forgiveness. Even as I was chasing him, honking the horn, I asked myself, *Can I find compassion for this person?* The obvious answer was, *Yes.* I still needed to read his license plate and still chose to press charges. But my anger was over in about ten minutes, and I never took his behavior personally. I just happened to be on the road at the same time as an enraged, drunk, out-of-control driver. As a result, I was mildly injured and mildly inconvenienced, but free.

Would I have blamed him if my injuries had been more severe? I don't know. I do know that I've held grudges for years against people for such offenses as not writing thank-you notes. There's a man on my swimming team who swims too close to my feet yet refuses to swim in front of me, and many days I struggle to forgive him for that. I don't think it's the magnitude of the offense that determines our response to it. I think it has more to do with our individual attitudes and beliefs—both of which can be gradually changed with practice, patience, and willingness to grant others the compassion we long for ourselves.

This no-blame path fascinates me, and now that I've noticed it in myself, I've also noticed it in others. Diana, the meeting planner who became a "whole person" and in the process forgave her parents and husband, says, "Now when people do mean things to me, I just feel sorry for them. My husband gets mad and wants me to get mad, but I realize that they can't help it."

"What if someone hurt your children?" I ask. The massacre at Columbine High School had taken place a few days before.

"I'm sure if anything happened to my children, like what just happened in Colorado, I would be like a wild lion and go after [the perpetrators]," she admits. "But I think in the end I would forgive them. When you are a whole person, there's no room to be judgmental.

"The other awesome thing is you can't do anything bad. If you even think about doing something wrong, your whole body says, *Don't go*

there, don't do that. So you never have to forgive anyone or ask for forgiveness. Any needs regarding forgiveness are all in the past. Then you
just go forward."

In retrospect, Diana can see that her mother, of all people, "had a clue
to becoming a whole person." The woman who never touched her, never
said she loved her, couldn't even hug her when she asked for it directly a
few years ago, used to tell her daughter, "Rise above it. That's how you
don't get hurt. You can't fix things. You have to rise above it, look down
on it, see it for what it really is."

As a child, Diana didn't understand. But she now sees the wisdom in
this advice and finds herself "rising above it" all the time.

It's possible that Jesus was talking about rising above it, or walking
along the no-blame path, in his parable about the return of the prodigal
son—though this is not the traditional interpretation. In this famous
story (Luke 15:11–32), a younger son asks his father for his inheritance,
then leaves home for a distant country, abandoning his family. There he
squanders his fortune. Humbled and hungry, he returns home, ready to
beg his father for a job.

The father, seeing his son in the distance, "was filled with compassion, and ran and put his arms around him and kissed him."

The son says, "Father, I have sinned against heaven and before you; I
am no longer worthy to be called your son; treat me like one of your
hired hands."

But the father asks his servants to bring the best robe and sandals and
to kill a fatted calf to celebrate the son's homecoming.

Jealous and angry, the older son complains that all his life he has
worked hard, been obedient, and neither asked for money nor squan-
dered it, yet unlike his younger brother, he has never received a party.

The father replies, "Son, you are always with me, and all that is mine
is yours. But we had to celebrate and rejoice, because this brother of
yours was dead and has come to life; he was lost and has been found."

Usually this is interpreted as a story about forgiveness, and through
that lens it's a wonderful story: The father forgives the younger son for
rudely asking for his inheritance, leaving home, and returning penniless.
He forgives the older son for his bitterness, reminding him, "You are
always with me."

But another interpretation was suggested to me by the therapist John Landi of Centerville, Virginia, who asked, "What if the father didn't blame the sons in the first place?"

At first I resisted Landi's line of thinking. I like the traditional interpretation of the parable. But when I reread it, I found no indication that the father had ever been angry or hurt by either son's behavior. So I considered this possibility: Maybe the father never blamed the sons. Maybe it's a story not about forgiveness but about unconditional love, about being "filled with compassion."

If this was Jesus's point—that the father loved wholly and unconditionally—then maybe the father is meant to represent God, not an exemplary human being. But on a human level, Landi's suggestion is tantalizing: What if we went directly to compassion, not blaming others in the first place?

If anyone understands how this process works, I think it's parents. Not all parents, but some of them.

I asked my own father: "Have you forgiven your children?"

"They've never given me anything to forgive them for," he responded immediately. Then, with his typical sense of humor, he added, "Either that or I've just got a faulty memory."

I pressed him, listing just a few of the obnoxious things my siblings and I have done.

"Oh, I never held any of that against you," he said matter-of-factly.

My friend Meredith Maran, trying to describe her love for her sons, told me, "You know how when a friend makes a big mistake but you keep supporting her because she's your friend and you love her? With your kids, it's like that except a hundred million times more so. It's not that they can't do anything bad. It's just that your love for them is far bigger than anything bad they could ever possibly do."

My friend Kimberly Carter is the mother of nine: three of her own children and six stepchildren. She's also the founder and director of a nonprofit homeless prevention project for teens called Above the Line. But since she's sort of Super-Mom, having mothered one set of kids or another for almost thirty years, I e-mailed her some questions about forgiveness in terms of her mothering. By happenstance, she and Becca, her teenager, had been talking about forgiveness the previous evening on their drive home from a musical. "I was saying that I have come to believe the clearest path to forgiveness is probably self-awareness," Kimberly wrote to me, "because I see how much I have needed to be forgiven. Knowing the blessing of having received that forgiveness makes me hesitate to withhold it from someone else."

She and Becca also "agreed that being heard seemed to be the prerequisite to forgiving."

In those few sentences, Kimberly touched on four of the five keys to forgiveness and freedom: awareness, validation, humility, and self-forgiveness. She then took my questions to her two oldest biological children: Becca, in her late teens, and Justin, in his early twenties, and the three of them came up with some more answers together. Here's her report on their discussion:

"We talked about how not forgiving is like being the 'keeper' of what someone did that wasn't okay, like a badge of remembering that I was right and they were wrong. So what if the other person blew it? We didn't have to be the keeper of that. That would keep us bound in the past, when the present was beckoning us to have a good time together. Justin and Becca said they always wanted to get along with each other more than they wanted to be right. It was so natural to be glad to see each other; it took energy to remember to be mad and not forgive each other. Deeper issues were resolved by talking, listening, and letting go of being right."

As a mother, Kimberly believes that forgiveness is necessary for her children's development. "Children are growing up daily, changing radically. If, as a mom, I hold on to who they were, and what they did, I deprive them of what they need most: spacious room to grow. Growing up necessarily includes bumping into boundaries, which is what transgressions are, I think, so forgiveness is a daily, ongoing process, a household tone."

She added that forgiveness seems natural in parenting. "I believe there is some intrinsic inclination to forgive one's children. Besides, what am I forgiving them for? It is guaranteed that children will learn by doing things 'wrong': hurting each other's feelings, taking what is not theirs. Parenting is all about keeping that in perspective, and certainly not getting uptight because my children do stupid or hurtful things and aren't understanding things they're not old enough to understand."

In teaching her children about forgiveness, she emphasizes self-forgiveness, she said, combined with compassion. "Know that you blew it, but that did not make you unlovable," she tells her children after they make a mistake. "Apologize readily, but don't get into self-loathing. Be gentle with yourself, take a bath, get a massage. By being kind to yourself, you set a tone of deserving love: your own love and the love of whomever you hurt.

"If you forgive yourself," she added, "you can forgive others, and both are essential parts of any relationship."

When I noticed that Kimberly had now spontaneously referred to all five of the keys to forgiveness and freedom, without my having told her the framework of this book, I smiled and mentioned to my longtime friend that apparently we were still in tune, though we now live far apart and see each other rarely. "The only thing you didn't mention is freedom," I said. "Is there any way you associate forgiveness with freedom?"

"It is always liberating to move out of the past," she replied immediately, "because you can always start over in the present. I guess that's where freedom comes in."

Imagine how freeing it would be to live in a family in which forgiveness is the norm. Not lenience, or low standards, or lack of responsibility, but openhearted forgiveness for all mistakes. Don't the best parents repeatedly offer their children this consistent love and affection despite the many ways that children can be hurtful, disappointing, and rude?

And when the roles are reversed, isn't it equally freeing for the parents when grown children forgive them? Don't all parents crave this: to be accepted and appreciated for their own best efforts despite their shortcomings?

Imagine an intimate relationship in which you know ahead of time that you will be forgiven. Aren't you likely to be more forthcoming about your own doubts, fears, and embarrassing behaviors? If you don't need to be ashamed or afraid, why wouldn't you admit that what you did was wrong, apologize for it, and discuss it honestly with your partner? Forgiveness enables people to be wholly themselves, without pretense.

I think this is exactly what we need: to feel forgiven, to feel permission to be human. I think it's when we experience this sort of forgiveness that we're most likely to allow our own creative, loving, and respectful selves to emerge. By contrast, it's harsh criticism and condemnation that contribute to low self-esteem, which is more likely to lead to reprehensible conduct.

Forgiveness can transform individuals and families and also entire cultures—as demonstrated most dramatically through the leadership of Nelson Mandela and Desmond Tutu. South Africa inaugurated Thabo Mbeki, its second democratically elected president, in 1999, bidding farewell to eighty-year-old Mandela. Patricia Mtsweni was one of thousands of South Africans attending the ceremony. She said of Mandela, "They put him in jail for twenty-seven years, and he forgave his jailers. They freed him, and he freed us, not just from the evil of apartheid, but from hatred."[1]

What if all religious groups, ethnic groups, and political groups forgave each other, freeing each other from hatred? "When I think of our world as a whole, and all the hate and violence in it, the concept of forgiving seems to be a big part of the answer," notes Maureen Vergara. "I see how essential forgiveness is for personal peace and freedom, and for interpersonal and international peace and freedom."

"Love your neighbors and pray for your persecutors," said Jesus. This is what Cardinal Bernardin did when he prayed for the man who falsely accused him of sexual abuse, it's what Father Jenco did when he prayed for his kidnappers, and it's what Linda Biehl did when she prayed for the men who murdered her daughter.

The Talmud counsels Jews to pray for their enemies and to help enemies before friends. The Indian saint Maharaji said, "Don't put anyone out of your heart." The message from these spiritual teachers seems to be to love everyone: our neighbors, our enemies, our friends, our parents, our kids. No matter how egregious the other person's behavior, don't put that person out of your heart. The person who closes her heart is the one who is hurt the most in that process.

But isn't it risky to have an open heart? To love everyone and anyone, including yourself? You can feel vulnerable walking around unguarded, heart thrust forward, without a shield. The Zen guide Cheri Huber says an open heart does not make a person vulnerable. In fact, she says, "the open heart is absolutely invulnerable because it accepts everything." We perceive ourselves to be vulnerable, she explains, only because "we're afraid we might not get what we want, we might not like what happens, or we might feel emotions we don't want to feel."

In the novel *Divine Secrets of the Ya-Ya Sisterhood,* Rebecca Wells writes, "The point is not *knowing* another person, or learning to *love* another person. The point is simply this: How tender can we bear to be? What good manners can we show as we welcome ourselves and others into our hearts?"[2]

How tender can we bear to be? What a wonderful question. It places the responsibility, and the choice, back on us.

It seems to me a fact of life that our hearts will sometimes close. I watch mine close almost daily as I silently criticize other people's behavior, distancing myself from them—as if I'm better, as if they're unworthy of my tenderness, love, compassion, and forgiveness. It hurts to do this, but I do it anyway. Despite my moments of transcendence, I've been criticizing and blaming people for many years and can't seem to give it up altogether, at least not yet.

But a reasonable daily goal, I believe, is to notice when the heart is closing, then open it again. Later, when it starts to close, notice that, then open it again.

And again.

I think it's in this process of noticing and opening and re-opening that freedom begins.

A Conversation with Mariah Burton Nelson

Q: *You have been writing about women and sports for twenty years. Now you have written a book about forgiveness. What was it like to write such a different sort of book?*

A: At first it felt risky, as new experiences often do. Yet it also felt totally natural and right, and that confirmed for me that it was a good decision. Usually I struggle with my writing, especially in terms of structure and research: I have trouble deciding what goes where (I want to put everything in the first chapter), and I have trouble deciding what to include and exclude. (I over-research a subject, then drown in my notes.) In this case, decisions about structure and research seemed obvious, and the writing just flowed. So either I'm finally learning how to write a book (which, of course, I hope is true!) or there was something about this subject matter that made the writing almost easy.

Q: *How did you do your research?*

A: As usual, I employed a combination of journalistic and scholarly techniques: books, magazines, newspapers, Internet sites, conferences, speeches, workshops, and original interviews with people I met along the way, was referred to, or sought through Internet lists. Because this was a new field for me, I wanted to make sure I wasn't missing anything, so I hired a research assistant from American University, Vera Gomes, who explored some of the physical and emotional benefits of forgiveness for chapter 3. For the more personal parts of the book, I did research on myself, so to speak, through therapy, discussions with friends, and journal-writing.

Q: *You mention the professional grudge-holder, the person who constantly complains about how unfair people have been to them (see chapter 2, "Why People Don't Forgive"). Is there any way to make this person see the light and become more forgiving?*

A: Probably not.

Q: *What if you want someone to forgive you and they won't? Is there anything you can do about that?*

A: You can apologize sincerely and repeatedly, without groveling. You can express concern about the damage done and offer to make amends however you can. You can promise not to do it again—if that's realistic. But none of that will necessarily have the desired effect. If it doesn't, you can try to forgive that person for not being able to forgive you. (If that's difficult, then you'll get a sense of how they might be struggling to forgive you!) And you can forgive yourself for whatever you did to them in the first place (which, of course, might also be difficult). In other words, when lack of forgiveness is causing pain, the best way to heal that pain is to summon as much compassion and forgiveness as you can, in all directions.

Q: *Did you get Bruce's permission to write the book? Does he even know about it?*

A: I didn't need his permission because it's my story. I haven't told him about it because we're not in contact. He has known since I was fourteen years old that I'm a writer, so he should not be terribly surprised when he finds out. Nor do I expect him to mind. I've kept his identity private, and I describe him as caring, kind, patient, and generous. Also, I don't think of this as a book "about" Bruce. It's about forgiveness. I might send him a copy. I haven't decided about that yet.

Q: *How do you feel about Bruce now?*

A: I still like the things I liked when I was young. I could even say I love him, in a different, more mature way. I'm not angry anymore.

Q: *By failing to identify Bruce, aren't you still protecting him? Isn't this just a reenactment of your childhood promise not to tell?*

A: I've given this a lot of thought. I deliberately live an open, honest life. But if I identified him, it could have negative consequences for him, and it could be misinterpreted as revenge on my part. When you forgive someone, you don't want any "further harm to come to him or his family," as Adam says in chapter 4 ("Awareness: The Courage to Inquire"). Because of my forgiveness process, I feel free. I want Bruce to feel free too, not burdened by my public airing of our past.

So I chose not to identify him. All things considered, this seemed like the wisest, most compassionate approach, but I realize I could be misunderstood or criticized either way.

Q: *There's so much talk about forgiveness these days. Are we developing a more forgiving culture?*

A: Not necessarily. But we're becoming more aware of the importance of forgiveness, and that's an important first step.

Q: *You quote from many religions in the book and seem to have an almost religious zeal for forgiveness. Do you think of forgiveness as a sort of spiritual path in itself?*

A: Yes. At least, I see it as a guiding principle, a light by which to see clearly. When I'm suffering, it's usually because I'm failing to be compassionate toward myself or others. Forgiving any of the parties involved can usually help me find my way to feeling more centered.

Q: *Can't forgiving people be taken advantage of?*

A: Yes. That's where boundaries come in. The wise, forgiving person does not allow herself to be used or abused. She says no—while keeping her heart open.

Q: *You have a successful career as an author and professional speaker. You're in a long-term relationship. You have good relationships with friends and family. You don't seem to have suffered much from Bruce's molestation. If you were damaged, where are the scars? If you can't point to alcoholism or severe depression, maybe it wasn't exploitation after all. Maybe you just got your heart broken.*

A: True, Bruce broke my heart. He also betrayed my friendship and violated my innocent body. People close to me know that there have been long-term negative effects, mostly related to trust and boundaries.

Q: *You said you were in love. Seems like maybe Bruce was in love too. What's wrong with that?*

A: I don't think adults should have sex with children. I feel strongly about that, not only because of my own experience, but because of extensive research and reading I've done on incest and childhood sexual abuse. I also strongly believe that adults should not have sex with people over whom they have power (coach-athlete, teacher-student, therapist-client), regardless of the age of the subservient person, and regardless of whether that person wants love, attention, sex, or all three. The authority figure must act responsibly and not sexualize the relationship.

For more information on this subject, I refer you to the "My Coach Says He Loves Me" chapter of *The Stronger Women Get, the More Men Love Football,* and also to *Sex in the Forbidden Zone* by Peter Rutter.

Q: *As you've mentioned in other books and articles, you're openly lesbian. Did you become a lesbian because of this early destructive relationship with Bruce?*

A: There's an old joke that if women became lesbians because of bad relationships with men, we'd all be lesbians. It's funny (to some people) because there's truth in it; childhood sexual abuse and other forms of abuse are distressingly common (though, of course, not all women have been abused). But as it turns out, most girls who were molested by men grow up to be heterosexual. Most boys who were molested by men grow up to be heterosexual too. There's no evidence that sexual orientation can be influenced by early sexual experiences.

Q: *You talk about freedom. Is it a place you get to, once and for all? Or are you describing a journey?*

A: I guess it's both. In any given moment, one might feel entirely free, as if one has arrived at a place called freedom. Then in the next moment, the heart closes again, and one must reforgive in order to become free again. So it's both a place and an ongoing journey.

Q: *Are there forgiveness support groups?*

A: Not yet, but why not start one? When people gather with the intent of becoming more forgiving, or simply the intent of exploring forgiveness, it's bound to lead to good things.

Reading Group Discussion Questions

- What are the advantages of being a forgiving person? Are there disadvantages?

- Are there times when you should not forgive? Are there times when you should not forgive yourself?

- Where did your beliefs or attitudes about forgiveness come from?

- How does this book compare to Nelson's first three books? Does she seem to have changed? If so, how?

- What does Nelson mean by freedom?

- Name a public figure who has apologized recently. How was this perceived? Name a public figure who has been openly forgiving. How was this perceived?

- In chapter 2, Nelson lists many reasons people don't forgive. Is there someone in your life whom you have not forgiven? If so, can you identify why not? Can you imagine how things might change if you did forgive them?

- In chapter 3, Nelson cites research showing that forgiveness decreases anxiety, depression, and anger and increases a sense of well-being, self-esteem, and hope. Have you experienced any sense of health or illness related to forgiveness or nonforgiveness?

- Some people quoted in the book have forgiven others for the most extreme crime imaginable: the murder of their children. What is your response when you contemplate that sort of forgiveness?

- In chapter 4, "Awareness: The Courage to Inquire," Stella, the adopted daughter, says, "The struggle was to let myself get angry in the first place." What's the relationship between anger and forgiveness? Do we have to get angry first?

- Nelson says in chapter 4 that blame is important: "You can't forgive someone until you know whom you blame. Often, women unthinkingly and irrationally blame themselves." Is this true of the women you know? Is there an ideal middle ground, somewhere between blaming others too little and blaming others too much?

- At one point, Nelson struggles with whether Bruce is "an evil child molester . . . or a nice guy who made a big mistake" (see chapter 6, "Compassion: Seeking the Humanity in Others"). What do you think? Did Bruce's letters influence your perspective on child molesters?

- Why do you think Nelson chose not to stay in contact with Bruce? (see chapter 11, "Reconciliation or Good-bye?"). What would you have done?

- In chapter 6, Nelson describes a dynamic she calls surrogate forgiveness: "extending compassion toward, and in a sense forgiving, someone close to the person who hurt you, or someone who symbolizes them in some way." Can you think of an example of surrogate forgiveness in your own life?

- In chapter 7 ("Humility: 'We Are All Struggling'"), Nelson quotes W. H. Auden: "You shall love your crooked neighbor / with your crooked heart." Is this a useful "commandment" for you? Why or why not?

- Do you forgive yourself on a regular basis? If so, how do you do that? What effect does this have on your life?

- Nelson makes a case for each of the five "keys to forgiveness and freedom" (awareness, validation, compassion, humility, and self-forgiveness) being "the most important." Which do you think is the most important? Which is the least important?

- In chapter 9 ("Apologies and Other Conditions: 'I'll Forgive You If . . .'"), Nelson notes that there are many meanings to "I'm sorry." What do you usually mean when you say it? If you don't often say "I'm sorry," what, if anything, keeps you from doing so?

- In chapter 10 ("Other Complications"), Nelson discusses a phenomenon she calls "Please forgive me and. . . ." What else do you notice that people usually want in addition to forgiveness?

- This is a book about interpersonal forgiveness. Can forgiveness have broader implications, beyond individual healing? In other words, what are the political and social implications? Do you see forgiveness happening in the world around you?

- Has this book changed your beliefs, behaviors, or ideas about forgiveness? If so, how?

Acknowledgments

I first became interested in forgiveness when Bruce asked me to forgive him. I am indebted to my former friend and coach for asking that question, and for his patience, kindness, honesty, and courage as we discussed emotional, spiritual, and deeply personal aspects of forgiveness.

I'm also indebted to the hundred or so people who allowed me to interview them, often about very painful subjects, for this book.

I'm grateful to my family members and friends for loving me unconditionally, especially as I struggled with rage, pain, and indecision related to my forgiveness process with Bruce. In particular, I would like to thank Kimberly Carter, Katherine Gekker, Mary Jo Kane, Marti Kovener, Barbara Logan, Carolyn Stone, and Lisa Voorhees for their wise and generous responses to my needs and questions.

Thanks to Tres Schnell for more than twenty-five years of deep friendship, and for inviting me to speak to the New Mexico teenagers of Project Respect.

Thanks to my good friends Meredith Maran and Ellen Wessel for reading and commenting on the entire manuscript.

For Margaret Coogan's compassion and clarity, I will be eternally grateful. I'm also grateful to my Zen teacher, Cheri Huber, for more than a dozen years of spiritual guidance. Terri Knapp, Nancy Davis, and Cordelia Anderson also offered therapeutic advice and support.

I'd also like to thank my friends Linda Bunker, Chris Cerf, Nancy Croteau, Lou Hawthorne, Nancy Hogshead, Nancy Kass, Deb Larkin, Ann Rasmussen, Morri Spang, and Lynne Waymon for their support of this project.

Thanks to Vera Gomes, my research assistant, who helped with the section on the psychological and physiological effects of forgiveness. Edith Bidwell, my personal assistant, handled e-mail and other overwhelming tasks on deadline.

Thanks to my friends and colleagues who sent articles or other relevant information: Kathleen Bashian, Alison Carlson, Val Cushman, Marie Earl, Suzanne Freedman, Jackson Katz, Madelyn Jennings, Kate Hays, Alane Mason, Walter McCabe, Becky Palmer, Colette Roberts, Susan Saidman, and Gail Whitaker.

I'm grateful to my editors, Caroline Pincus and Liz Perle, for understanding and embracing this book from the beginning; to my lecture agents, Kevin Moore and Jayne Moore, for creating opportunities for me to speak on this subject and others; and to my longtime literary agent, Felicia Eth, for representing me well for more than a dozen years, for believing in me, and for helping me create an extremely rewarding career.

Notes

CHAPTER 1: MY YEAR OF FORGIVING DANGEROUSLY

1. I have chosen to use a pseudonym because I do not believe he is molesting other girls, because I have come to respect him and his desire for privacy, because I do not wish any further harm to come to him or his family, and, perhaps most important, because this book is not about Bruce. It's about forgiveness and freedom. Several other interview subjects were also given pseudonyms to protect their privacy. All of these people are identified by first names only.

2. For more information about the International Forgiveness Institute, write to P. O. Box 6153, Madison, WI 53716–0153, or visit their Web site at www.forgiveness-institute.org.

3. C. S. Lewis, *Mere Christianity: Comprising the Case for Christianity, Christian Behaviour, and Beyond Personality* (New York: Touchstone Books, 1996).

4. Hannah Arendt, *The Human Condition* (Chicago: University of Chicago Press, 1958), p. 237, cited in Doris Donnelly, *Learning to Forgive* (New York: Macmillan, 1979), pp. 10–11.

5. Desmond Tutu, National Conference on Forgiveness, University of Wisconsin, Madison, Wisconsin, 1995.

6. Simon Wiesenthal et al., *Sunflower: On the Possibilities and Limits of Forgiveness* (New York: Schocken Books, 1998).

7. Quoted in Patricia Raybon, *My First White Friend: Confessions on Race, Love, and Forgiveness* (New York: Penguin, 1997), p. 129.

CHAPTER 2: WHY PEOPLE DON'T FORGIVE

1. Doris Donnelly, *Learning to Forgive* (New York: Macmillan, 1979), pp. 10–11.

2. His Holiness the Dalai Lama, *The Good Heart: A Buddhist Perspective on the Teachings of Jesus* (Boston: Wisdom Publications, 1996), p. 15.

3. Peter Rutter, *Sex in the Forbidden Zone: When Men in Power—Therapists, Doctors, Clergy, Teachers, and Others—Betray Women's Trust* (Los Angeles: Jeremy Tarcher, 1986), p. 186.

4. Henri J. M. Nouwen, *The Return of the Prodigal Son: A Story of Homecoming* (New York: Image Books, 1994), pp. 129, 130.

5. Reuter News Service, "Dallas Bishop Apologizes to Victims of Sexual Assault," *Washington Post,* July 28, 1997, p. A4.

6. Lois Romano, "Arkansas Pair Found Guilty of Five Slayings," *Washington Post,* August 12, 1998, p. A3.

7. Shirley Povitch, "Blood, Sweat, and Jeers," *Washington Post,* July 3, 1997, p. C1.

CHAPTER 3: WHY FORGIVE?

1. Quoted in Donnelly, *Learning to Forgive.*

2. Suzanne R. Freedman and Robert D. Enright, "Forgiveness as an Intervention Goal with Incest Survivors," *Journal of Consulting and Clinical Psychology* 64, no. 8 (1996): 983–91.

3. J. H. Hebl and Robert D. Enright, "Forgiveness as a Psychotherapeutic Goal with Elderly Females," *Psychotherapy* 30 (1993): 658–67; Radhi H. Al-Mabuk, Robert D. Enright, and Paul Cardis, "A Forgiveness Education Program with Parentally Love-Deprived Late Adolescents," *Journal of Moral Education* 24, no. 4 (1995); and Freedman and Enright, "Forgiveness as an Intervention Goal."

4. Al-Mabuk, Enright, and Cardis, "A Forgiveness Education Program."

5. Catherine T. Coyle and Robert D. Enright, "Forgiveness Intervention with Postabortion Men," *Journal of Consulting and Clinical Psychology* 65, no. 4 (1977): 1042–46.

6. Freedman and Enright, "Forgiveness as an Intervention Goal," p. 983.

7. Daniel Zwerdling, National Public Radio, April 26, 1997, from the NPR Archives of 1998.

8. Scott Heller, "Emerging Field of Forgiveness Studies Explores How We Let Go of Grudges," *Chronicle of Higher Education,* July 17, 1998.

9. Oscar Hijuelos, *Mr. Ives' Christmas* (New York: HarperPerennial, 1996), pp. 172–74, 193.

10. Azim Khamisa, with Carl Goldman, *Azim's Bardo: A Father's Journey from Murder to Forgiveness* (Los Altos, Calif.: Rising Star Press, 1998).

11. Tom Spanbauer, *The Man Who Fell in Love with the Moon* (New York: HarperPerennial, 1992).

12. Wes Crenshaw and Greg Tangari, "The Apology: Creating a Bridge Between Remorse and Forgiveness," *Family Therapy Networker* (November-December 1998): 32–37.

13. Debbie Morris, *Forgiving the Dead Man Walking* (Grand Rapids, Mich.: Zondervan, 1998), pp. 180, 249–50.

14. Helen Prejean, *Dead Man Walking* (New York: Vintage Books, 1993).

15. Lawrence Martin Jenco, *Bound to Forgive: Pilgrimages in Time and Mind* (Notre Dame, Ind.: Ave Maria Press, 1993).

16. Ibid.

17. This quote is from the New Revised Standard Version. Older versions (King James, Revised Standard Version, and others) imply that Jesus says she has been forgiven because she has loved much. "Therefore I tell you, her sins, which are many, are forgiven, for she loved much."

18. Heller, "Emerging Field of Forgiveness Studies."

Chapter 4: Awareness

1. Judith Herman, *Trauma and Recovery: The Aftermath of Violence—From Domestic Abuse to Political Terror* (New York: Basic Books, 1997), p. 243.

Chapter 5: Validation

1. Quoted in Robin Casarjian, *Forgiveness and Other Acts of Love* (New York: Bantam, 1992), p. 50.

Chapter 6: Compassion

1. Bernhard Schlink, *The Reader* (New York: Vintage, 1995), p. 157.

2. Quoted in Robin Casarjian, *Forgiveness: A Bold Choice for a Peaceful Heart* (New York: Bantam Books, 1992), p. 45.

3. Laura Parker, "Nine Years After Bus Tragedy, the Healing Goes On," *USA Today,* July 3, 1997, p. 13A.

4. Deborah Morris, *Forgiving the Dead Man Walking* (Grand Rapids, Mich.: Zondervan, 1998).

5. Ibid., pp. 198–99.

6. Ibid., p. 162.

7. His Holiness the Dalai Lama, *The Good Heart: A Buddhist Perspective on the Teachings of Jesus* (Boston: Wisdom Publications, 1996), p. 49.

8. *The Compendium of Practices,* cited in ibid.

9. Quoted in Doris Donnelly, *Learning to Forgive* (New York: Macmillan, 1979), p. 50.

10. Quoted in ibid., p. 56.

Chapter 7: Humility

1. Quoted in Kathleen Norris, *The Cloister Walk* (New York: Riverhead Books, 1996), p. 274.

2. Alcoholics Anonymous, *Twelve Steps and Twelve Traditions* (Alcoholics Anonymous World Service, Inc., Box 459, Grand Central Station, New York, NY 10163), p. 78.

3. Robert Bly, *The Kabir Book: Forty-four of the Ecstatic Poems of Kabir: Versions by Robert Bly* (Boston: Beacon Press, 1971), p. 57.

4. Nuala O'Faolain, *Are You Somebody?: The Accidental Memoir of a Dublin Woman* (New York: Owl Books, 1999), p. 214.

5. Jack Kornfield, *A Path with Heart: A Guide Through the Perils and Promises of Spiritual Life* (New York: Bantam Books, 1993), p. 267.

6. Ibid.

7. Lawrence Martin Jenco, *Bound to Forgive: Pilgrimages in Time and Mind* (Notre Dame, Ind.: Ave Maria Press, 1993).

8. Alcoholics Anonymous, *Twelve Steps and Twelve Traditions* (Alcoholics Anonymous World Service, Inc., Box 459, Grand Central Station, New York, NY 10163), p. 91.

9. Ibid., p.78.

CHAPTER 8: SELF-FORGIVENESS

1. Beverly Flanigan, *Forgiving Yourself* (New York: Macmillan, 1996), p. 188.

2. Debbie Morris, *Forgiving the Dead Man Walking* (Grand Rapids, Mich.: Zondervan, 1998), p. 224.

3. Sogyal Rinpoche, *The Tibetan Book of Living and Dying* (San Francisco: HarperSanFrancisco, 1993), p. 213.

4. Robert Bly, *The Kabir Book: Forty-four of the Ecstatic Poems of Kabir: Versions by Robert Bly* (Boston: Beacon Press, 1971), p. 57.

5. Jack Kornfield, *A Path with Heart: A Guide Through the Perils and Promises of Spiritual Life* (New York: Bantam Books, 1993), p. 286.

CHAPTER 9: APOLOGIES AND OTHER CONDITIONS

1. Quoted in Scott Heller, "Emerging Field of Forgiveness Studies Explores How We Let Go of Grudges," *Chronicle of Higher Education*, July 17, 1998.

2. Janis Abrahms Spring, *After the Affair: Healing the Pain and Rebuilding Trust When a Partner Has Been Unfaithful* (New York: HarperCollins, 1996), p. 238.

3. Judith Herman, *Trauma and Recovery: The Aftermath of Violence—From Domestic Abuse to Political Terror* (New York: Basic Books, 1997), p. 190.

4. Jonathan R. Cohen, "Advising Clients to Apologize," *Southern California Law Review* 72 (1999): p. 1019.

5. Miss Manners, "Sorry," *Washington Post*, August 3, 1997, p. D2.

6. Fred Bayles, "Au Pair 'Saddened' by Child's Death," *USA Today*, November 12, 1997, p. A1.

7. David Gelernter, "How I Survived the Unabomber," *Time*, September 22, 1997, p. 86, excerpted from David Gelernter, *Drawing Life: Surviving the Unabomber* (New York: Free Press, 1997).

8. Robert Macy, "Killer Pleads for Forgiveness Before Getting Life Sentence," *USA Today*, October 15, 1998, p. 9A.

9. James B. Simpson, *Simpson's Contemporary Quotations* (Boston: Houghton Mifflin, 1988), p. 33.

10. Deborah Tannen, *The Argument Culture: Stopping America's War of Words* (New York: Ballantine Books, 1998).

11. Dennis Prager, "Day of Reckoning," *Wall Street Journal,* September 25, 1998.

12. Deborah E. Lipstadt, quoted in Simon Wiesenthal et al., *The Sunflower: On the Possibilities and Limits of Forgiveness* (New York: Schocken Books, 1998), p. 195.

13. Alcoholics Anonymous, *Twelve Steps and Twelve Traditions* (Alcoholics Anonymous World Service, Inc., Box 459, Grand Central Station, New York, NY 10163), p. 86.

CHAPTER 10: OTHER COMPLICATIONS

1. José Hobday, quoted in Simon Wiesenthal et al., *The Sunflower: On the Possibilities and Limits of Forgiveness* (New York: Schocken Books, 1998).

2. Eric Pooley, "Death or Life?" *Time,* June 16, 1977, p. 31.

3. Daniel Zwerdling, National Public Radio, April 26, 1997.

4. Associated Press, "Son of Sam Says He Deserves to Die, Is Sorry," *USA Today,* August 4, 1997, p. A1.

5. Ceci Connolly, "Gore, Clinton Face Toughest Loyalty Test," *Washington Post,* June 16, 1999, A1.

6. Ella Higginson, "Wearing out Love," in *The Columbia Dictionary of Quotations* (New York: Columbia University Press, 1995).

7. Peter Rutter, *Sex in the Forbidden Zone* (Los Angeles: Jeremy Tarcher, 1986), p. 186.

8. Ellen Bass and Laura Davis, *The Courage to Heal: A Guide for Women Survivors of Child Sexual Abuse* (New York: HarperPerennial Library), pp. 149, 151.

9. Marita Golden, *Saving Our Sons* (New York: Anchor Books, 1996).

CHAPTER 11: RECONCILIATION OR GOOD-BYE?

1. Quoted in Anne Gearan, "Cruelty of War Finds Peace in Forgiveness," *San Francisco Chronicle,* April 13, 1997, p. A1.

2. Cardinal Joseph Bernardin, *The Gift of Peace: Personal Reflections* (Chicago: Loyola Press, 1997), p. 23.

3. Ibid., pp. 25–26.

4. Ibid., p. 31.

5. David W. Schell, *Forgiveness Therapy* (St. Meinrad, Ind.: Abbey Press, 1993).

6. Richard Hoffman, *Half the House* (New York: Harcourt Brace, 1995), p. 139.

CHAPTER 12: FREEDOM

1. Jon Jeter, "In South Africa, a President Replaces an Icon," *Washington Post,* June 17, 1999, p. A1.

2. Rebecca Wells, *Divine Secrets of the Ya-Ya Sisterhood* (New York: HarperCollins, 1997).

Index